AMISTAD NATIONAL RECREATION AREA

TEXAS

WATER RESOURCES SCOPING REPORT

Carol E. Purchase[1], David Larson[2,] Mark D. Flora[3] and John Reber[4]

Technical Report NPS/NRWRD/NRTR-2001/295

September, 2001

[1]National Park Service, Big Bend National Park, Texas
[2]National Park Service, Amistad National Recreation Area, Del Rio, Texas
[3]Water Resources Division, National Park Service, Fort Collins, Colorado
[4]Intermountain Support Office, National Park Service, Denver, Colorado

United States Department of the Interior
National Park Service

Table of Contents

TABLES

FIGURES

EXECUTIVE SUMMARY

Amistad Reservoir is an immense water area on the Texas-Mexico border near the city of Del Rio in Val Verde County, Texas. The reservoir was created under the provisions of the Water Treaty of 1944 between the United States of America and Mexico, and Public Law 86-605, (July 7, 1960) which authorized the joint construction of the international storage dam, to be managed by the International Boundary and Water Commission (IBWC). At normal water level the reservoir has 65,000 surface acres (26,299 hectares) of water, with 43,250 acres (17,499 hectares) in the United States and 21,750 acres (8,800 hectares) in Mexico.

On November 11, 1965 the IBWC, by Memorandum of Agreement, assigned administration of all U.S. lands and surface waters of the reservoir (57,292 acres, 23,180 hectares) to the National Park Service (NPS) to provide for recreation management. On November 28, 1990, Congress established Amistad National Recreation Area (NRA) as a unit of the NPS system to provide for outdoor recreation use of the reservoir and to protect the scenic, scientific, cultural and other values contributing to public enjoyment of these lands and waters (PL 101-628).

Most of the regional recreational needs for fishing, scuba diving, boating, swimming, picnicking, camping, and hunting are met by Amistad NRA. Tourists are also attracted by these recreational opportunities, thereby augmenting the local economy. The reservoir is known as a prime location for bass fishing, and large fishing tournaments are frequently held at the reservoir.

This report summarizes the available information concerning water resources in the area. The activities of other water related state and federal agencies are described, along with current water quality monitoring programs and studies. The major issues related to water resources are described in detail.

Water resources at conservation pool include the 65,000 surface acre (26,299 hectares) reservoir along with 6 river miles (9.7 kilometers (km)) of the Rio Grande, 3 river miles (4.8 km) of the Pecos River, and 2.7 miles (4.3 km) of the Devils River. The Devils River is relatively pristine with high scenic and recreational value. Native riparian vegetation has not been replaced by exotic species and the river is largely unregulated, making this river unique in West Texas.

Springs constitute an important water resource at Amistad National Recreation Area both by serving as a source of almost a third of the water entering the reservoir and supporting critical aquatic and riparian habitat types in this arid environment.

The major water resource issues center around two primary factors: the declining water quantity and quality of the Rio Grande and the Pecos Rivers and the effects of fluctuating reservoir levels.

Declining water quality and flows in the Rio Grande are degrading reservoir water quality and impacting park operations. Salinity levels in the reservoir are increasing rapidly and may increase to the point of significantly altering the aquatic life in the reservoir and the

1

ability of the water to be used for downstream irrigation. Some trace elements, such as mercury, are also on the rise, which may by partially due to atmospheric deposition.

Reservoir levels have been fluctuating from 30 feet (9 meters (m)) to over 50 vertical feet (15 m) below the conservation pool level since 1994, which has affected boat ramps, swim beaches and other facilities. In addition to increasing workloads for Amistad NRA staff, the fluctuating reservoir levels affect archeological sites, threatened and endangered species and visitor access.

Another concern is the potential for hazardous spills into the reservoir. With the highway and railroad bridge, in addition to the several marinas located on the reservoir, a spill control and prevention plan is essential.

Recommendations in this report include:

- Increased participation in The Texas Clean Rivers water quality monitoring program, specifically for the Devil's and Pecos Rivers.

- Develop a spring protection strategy and design an inventory and long-term monitoring program for critical spring sites.

- Support the development of a bi-national fisheries management plan.

- Enhance interagency relationships for developing research proposals focussed upon water-related synoptic research studies identified throughout this scoping process.

- Assess the potential of current and potential development / land use change in the Devils River watershed on sensitive park resources.

- Develop a parkwide spill prevention control and counter-measure plan.

- Assess the effects of sedimentation on visitor facilities.

- Survey for and initiate cooperative efforts for the control of exotic species.

- Survey for karst features found on park lands.

- Acquire complete knowledge of water quantity issues to be faced over the next 20 years.

- Assess the effects of motorized vessels on park resources.

The NRA should strongly consider increasing natural resource staff to include a water resource position to aid in the coordinating and implementing of water quality monitoring and research programs. Many different national and state agencies are involved in monitoring, researching and resolving water resource issues in the Amistad NRA area, creating many cooperative opportunities for work on these issues.

ACKNOWLEDGMENTS

The Amistad National Recreation Area Water Resources Scoping Report was a collaborative effort among National Park Service staff members assigned to Amistad NRA, Big Bend National Park, NPS Intermountain Region's Support Office, and the NPS Water Resources Division. In addition to the primary authors several individuals within these offices contributed specific sub-sections of the report. The primary authors would like to express their sincere appreciation to Barry Long (Water Operations Branch, NPS Water Resources Division) for the sub-section pertaining to the proposed Dryden Hazardous Waste Landfill issue, Eric Lord (Colorado State University/Water Rights Branch, NPS Water Resources Division) for the sub-section discussing water rights and Gary Smillie (Water Operations Branch, NPS Water Resources Division) for the sub-section relating to floodplain issues.

In addition the authors would like to thank our colleagues who provided important information used in developing this report. These include Bill Jeffers (IBWC); Carlos Rubinstein and Christine Kolbe (TNRCC); Chuck Lorea (San Antonio River Authority); Dee Lurry and Bruce Moring (USGS); Jimmy Dean, Joe Kraai, and Robert Howells (TPWD); Chris Butler (Amistad NRA); Marco A. Ramos Frayjo (SEMARNAT); and Daniel Hernandez Montoya (Instituto Nacional de la Pesca).

Finally, we would like to thank our internal reviewers including Barry Long, Gary Smillie and Dan McGlothlin (NPS Water Resources Division) as well as Bill Sontag (former Superintendent Amsitad NRA) and Todd Brindle (Acting Superintendent Amistad NRA) for their interest and support leading to the completion of this report. Photographs were taken by John Reber, except for Figures 4 and 5 which were taken by Cheri McEwen of Amistad NRA. Park map was provided by Chris Butler of Amistad NRA.

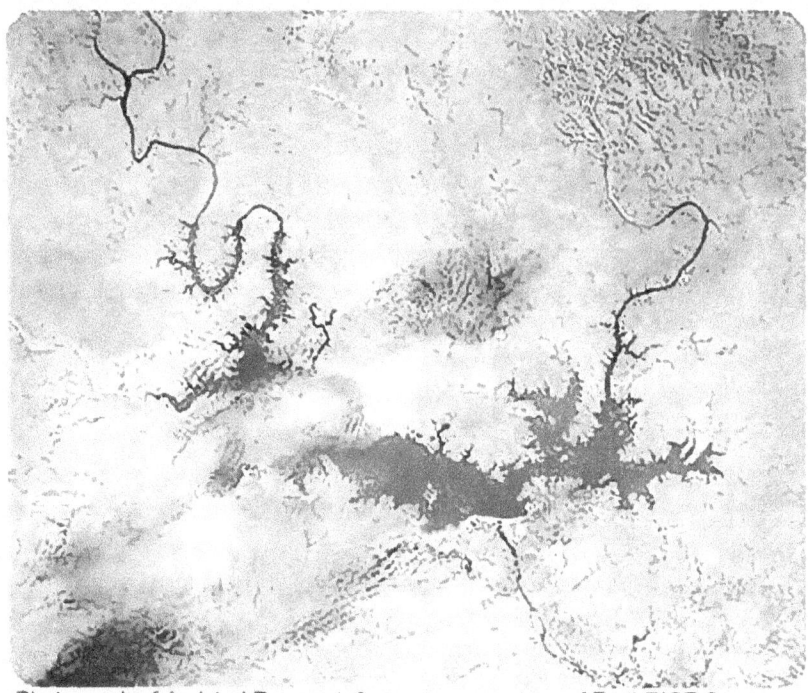

Photograph of Amistad Reservoir from space courtesy of EarthRISE Space Shuttle Photographs. (http://www.hevanet.com/landlope/earthrise.htm)

INTRODUCTION

Amistad National Recreation Area (NRA) is an international recreation area on the United States - Mexico Border, created as a result of the Treaty of February 3, 1944[1], which authorized building Amistad Dam. Amistad Reservoir was completed in November 1969, at a cost of $74 million. It was built to take advantage of water storage opportunities at the confluence of the Devils River, the Rio Grande, and the Pecos River near Del Rio Texas. Amistad Reservoir occupies much of the southern boundary of Val Verde County, Texas and many miles of the shoreline of the Rio Grande, Devils, and Pecos Rivers.

Many dams, reservoirs, and irrigation withdrawals in the U.S. and Mexico affect the Rio Grande throughout its 1,885 mile (3033 kilometer (km)) course from Colorado to the Gulf of Mexico. Amistad Reservoir is but one of these; primarily storing water for downstream irrigation demands from the U.S. Bureau of Reclamation's Falcon International Reservoir, providing flood control, generating electric power through its dam, and finally, providing recreational opportunities throughout Amistad NRA.

Amistad NRA provides opportunities for fishing, boating, camping, and swimming. Fishing is a major use of the reservoir. Recreational fisherman from both sides of the border use the reservoir, in addition to frequent Bass tournaments on the U.S. side, and commercial fishing on the Mexican side of the reservoir.

The purpose of this report is to provide an overview of the water resources of Amistad NRA. Information was gathered from the staff of Amistad NRA, the many state and federal agencies working within this reach of the Rio Grande, as well as from available scientific literature. Current water quality monitoring programs and studies by other agencies have been identified in the section on water quality. Internet sites with water quality and flow data relevant to Amistad NRA are listed at the end of the report. The major water resource issues have been identified and summarized, with recommendations listed for further research and monitoring efforts.

Legislative / Operational framework

Although Amistad NRA manages the surface water and land surrounding the reservoir on the United States side, the operation of the dam and allocation of the waters are subject to a variety of state, federal and international laws and treaties. This section explains the various laws and agencies that play a role in managing the water resources within this NRA.

---

[1] Utilization of Waters of the Colorado and Tijuana Rivers and of the Rio Grande, Treaty Between the United States of America and Mexico, February 3, 1944. (59 Stat. 1219, TS 455). Referred to as 'Treaty of 1944'.

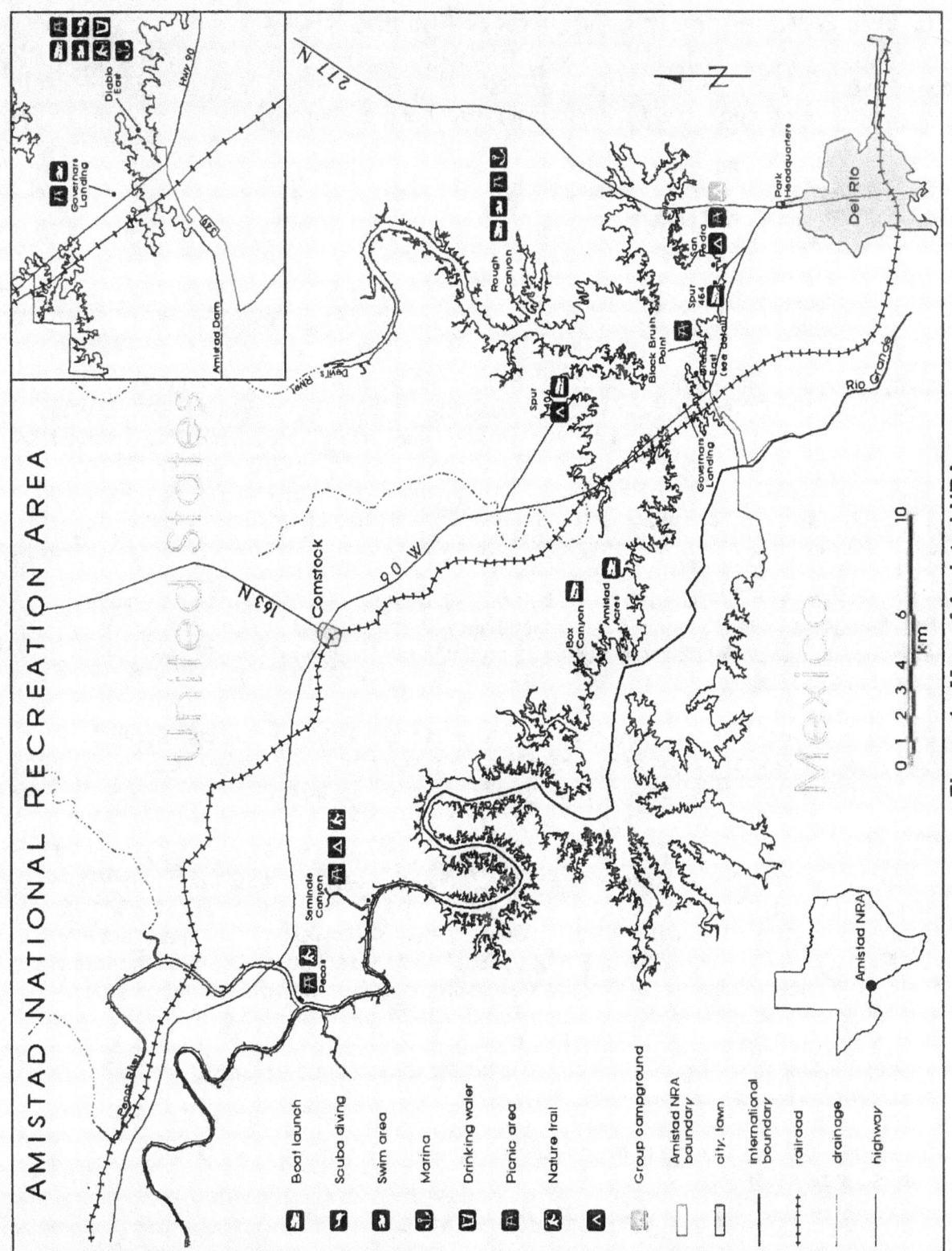

Figure 1. Map of Amistad NRA

5

Purpose & Management Objectives of Amistad NRA

The Treaty of 1944 authorized the construction of Amistad Dam (Figure 2), which was completed in 1969 by the United States and Mexico. Article 3 of this treaty provides for joint use of international waters in the following order of precedence:

1. Domestic and municipal use
2. Agriculture and stock raising
3. Electric power generation
4. Other industrial uses
5. Navigation
6. Fishing and hunting
7. Other beneficial uses which may be determined by the Commission[2].

A 1965 Memorandum of Agreement between the International Boundary and Water Commission (IBWC) (United States Section) and the National Park Service[3] (NPS) directs the NPS to administer all land and surface water on the United States side of the reservoir, except for areas required by the IBWC for dam operations. The IBWC is responsible for administration and operation of the dam. The memorandum states that the NPS is to manage the area with "consideration for the best possible use of the reservoir and adjacent areas for recreational enjoyment by the public."

Amistad NRA was established to "provide for public outdoor recreation use and enjoyment of the lands and waters associated with the United States portion... of Lake Amistad Reservoir," and to protect "scenic, scientific, and cultural... value(s)" (Public Law 101-682, November 28, 1990).

To this end, Amistad NRA is managed to enhance recreational opportunities. Public facilities including boat ramps, docks, campgrounds, and picnic areas have been developed and are maintained at various locations around the lake.

Visitor Use

Approximately one million people per year visit Amistad NRA. About 85% come for water-based recreational activities; the rest use camping and day use facilities. About 2/3 of all visitors are considered 'regional' visitors. They are from southwestern Texas and southern New Mexico; Del Rio, San Antonio, San Angelo, Midland/Odessa, Hobbs; and other area locations. The remainder are destination visitors from other areas, and 'through' visitors travelling in west Texas and stopping at Amistad NRA on the way.

Except for visitors stopping to utilize camping facilities, most people come to Amistad NRA because of the water recreation in the reservoir.

Table 1 provides an example of the use-levels found at the campgrounds and from boaters on the reservoir.

---

[2] International Boundary and Water Commission
[3] Memorandum of Agreement between The United States Section, International Boundary and Water Commission and The National Park Service Relating to the Development and Administration of Recreation on the United States Side of Amistad International Dam and Reservoir. Signed November 11, 1965.

Table 1. Campground and Boating Use Levels.

Year	Campground Overnight Stays	Boat Trailers
1990	22,379	63,878
1991	38,922	140,973
1992	38,571	181,882
1993	40,211	182,318
1994	34,713	222,188
1995	30,199	212,322
1996	24,210	151,154
1997	26,333	119,810
1998	20,286	123,807
1999	21,237	127,222

This information is taken from the Monthly Public Use Report, EZ-Forms Database program , NPS.

Compacts and Treaties

Several compacts and treaties affect the upstream distribution of water on the Rio Grande and the Pecos River. These laws and agreements distribute the majority of water from these rivers to upstream users, significantly decreasing the amount of water entering Amistad Reservoir.

1906 Treaty

The first allocation of the Rio Grande dates back to 1906. The United States is obligated under the 1906 Water Convention[4] to deliver 60,000 acre-feet[5] (ac-ft) (2613.6 million cubic meters) of water to Mexico from the Rio Grande above El Paso. This water is delivered to the Mexican canal (just upstream of the City of Juarez, Mexico) with a schedule of deliveries to provide the majority of the water during the growing season (March to September). In return for this water, Mexico waived all rights to waters originating between the Mexican Canal and Fort Quitman, TX, approximately 75 miles (121 km) downstream of El Paso.

Rio Grande Compact Commission

In 1923, the Rio Grande Compact Commission was formed, with a compact ratified in 1939. This agreement allocates the flow in the Rio Grande between the States of Colorado, New Mexico and Texas. The Bureau of Reclamation holds that all of the water in the Rio Grande from Elephant Butte Dam, New Mexico to Fort Quitman, Texas, is appropriated for use of the Rio Grande Project and so disposes of this water through contracts with the Elephant Butte Irrigation District, the El Paso County Water Improvement District and other entities (Niemi and McGuckin, 1997).

As a result of this policy, only a small amount of water from the upper Rio Grande Basin actually flows below Ft. Quitman and is primarily the result of local summer rainfall runoff and industrial and municipal wastewater effluent disharges in the El Paso / Juarez area. Approximately half of this water is lost prior to reaching Presidio, Texas. The river channel

---

[4] Convention between the United States and Mexico, Equitable Distribution of the Waters of the Rio Grande, May 21, 1906. (34 Stat. 2953, TS 455).

[5] A measurement unit commonly used to describe large volumes of water, an acre-foot (ac-ft) is the amount of water spread over one acre, at a depth of one foot and is equivalent to 325,851 gallons.

below Ft. Quitman is poorly defined due to a lack of high flows to maintain a stream channel. An exotic tree, salt cedar (*Tamarix spp.*) lines the river channel, transpiring great amounts of water, further decreasing the flow below Frt. Quitman. Thus the majority of water, which flows into Amistad Reservoir from the Rio Grande, originates either in the Rio Conchos in Mexico or results from rainfall runoff along the river between Presidio and Amistad Reservoir.

Treaty of February 3, 1944

Applicable downstream of Fort Quitman, this 1944 treaty between the United States and Mexico, allocates water from both the mainstem of the Rio Grande and from specific named tributaries. This treaty also authorized the construction of three international reservoirs, including Amistad Reservoir.

Several creeks flowing into the Rio Grande from the north are allocated entirely to the United States. The Pecos River and Goodenough Spring (inundated by Amistad Reservoir) are two perennial inflows to Amistad Reservoir, which are also allocated entirely to the United States.

The flow from six tributaries flowing into the Rio Grande from Mexico are allocated two-thirds to Mexico and one-third to the United States Of these six tributaries, only the Rio Conchos is located upstream of Amistad Reservoir.

The United States is entitled to a minimum of 350,000 ac-ft (431.721 million cubic meters) annually from these 6 tributaries, averaged over a 5 year cycle. In the case of drought or other conditions, under which Mexico cannot deliver this volume of water, the deficit is to be made up during the following 5 year cycle.

A five year cycle is ended early and all deficits are absolved whenever the conservation capacities assigned to the United States of both Amistad and Falcon Reservoirs are filled; such as can occasionally occur as a result of hurricanes or tropical storms.

For the period of 1984 to 1997, only two cycles ran to completion (1982 - 1987 and 1992 - 1997), the remaining cycles ended when both Amistad and Falcon Reservoirs were filled as a result of large storms (NPS, 1999c).

As the water deficit can be resolved through the filling of the reservoirs from storms or from supplying more water from tributaries downstream of Amistad Reservoir, a steady supply of water from the Rio Grande is not guaranteed. This can result in prolonged low lake levels unrelated to climatic drought conditions. Downstream of Amistad, the reduced flows have resulted in the Rio Grande no longer reaching the Gulf of Mexico. Exotic aquatic plants, hydrilla and water hyacinth, flourish in the low flows and now clog the river channel below Falcon Reservoir.

During the cycle 1992 to 1997, the average 1/3 of annual flow, the amount allocated to the United States was only 144,819 ac-ft (178.790 million cubic meters), which is about 40% of the minimum required. This deficit can be resolved with through increased flows from Mexican tributaries during the current 5 year cycle (1998-2002), or from transferring Mexican water stored in Amistad Reservoir and Falcon to the United States

Pecos River Compact

The Pecos River Compact, a 1948 agreement between New Mexico and Texas, gives Texas the same amount of water each year as it received in 1947. Each state has the right to half the floodwaters in a given year. The compact also authorizes additional reservoirs as needed to utilize unappropriated water and projects designed to reduce salinity.

Reservoir Operations

Virtually, all of the water within the Amistad Reservoir is owned by downstream State of Texas water rights holders and the Mexican Government. Generally, Amistad Reservoir works in tandem with Falcon Reservoir, which is located 340 river miles (547 km) downstream from Amistad Dam. About 95% of the water released from Amistad Reservoir passes through to Falcon Reservoir for use in the Lower Rio Grande valley. The only primary withdrawals between Amistad Reservoir and Falcon are for municipal use by the cities of Ciudad Acuna, Piedras Negras, Eagle Pass, Laredo, and Nuevo Laredo, and agricultural use by water rights holders downstream of Del Rio (Bill Jeffers, IBWC, pers. comm., 1999).

Falcon Reservoir can store about 3 million ac-ft (3.7 billion cubic meters) of water, and United States deliveries from Amistad Reservoir to Falcon Reservoir are controlled by the Texas Natural Resources Conservation Commission's (TNRCC) Watermaster in Harlingen, TX. Domestic/municipal & industrial users receive the highest priority with a reserve set aside of 225,000 ac-ft (277 million cubic meters) re-established each month for these uses. Following this in priority is an operational reserve of 150,000 ac-ft (185 million cubic meters) which is utilized by the TNRCC to compensate for evaporative, conveyance, and seepage losses and adjustments. The remainder of the United States allocation is available for agricultural use and mining (Carlos Rubinstein, TNRCC, pers. comm., 2000).

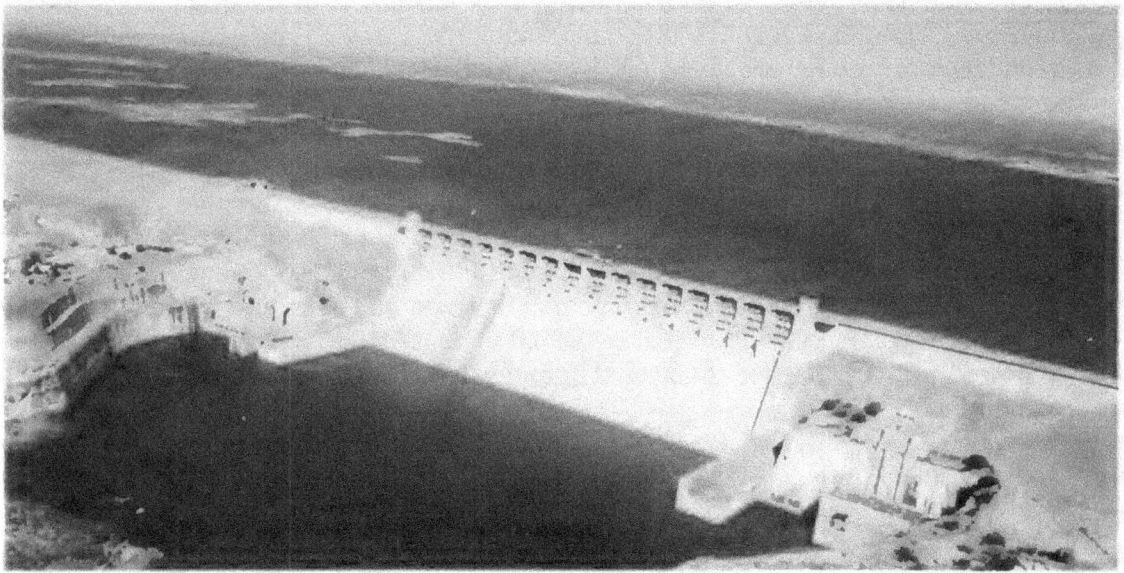

Figure 2. Amistad Dam

Mexican deliveries are regulated by the Comision Nacional del Aqua (CNA) of the Mexican government. The TNRCC and CNA, in turn, respond to the water rights requirements to meet the needs of the irrigation districts/irrigators with heavy periods of irrigation in the Lower Rio Grande valley typically occurring in January, in April/May, and if water is available, often in September. Important determinations regarding water short falls and agricultural water rights deliveries for the upcoming growing seasons are generally made in October (Bill Jeffers, IBWC, pers. comm., 1999). A lot has been learned over the last several years of regional drought and reduced water deliveries, with irrigators sometimes shifting to less water intensive crops and sometimes opting not to plant a spring crop (Bill Jeffers, IBWC, pers. comm., 1999).

In addition, there are a number of other operational issues, which tend to influence discharges from Amistad Reservoir. These include:

- Amistad Reservoir was designed as a multipurpose project with considerations given to water supply, flood control, hydroelectric generation and recreational usage. In order to provide adequate flood control, the "conservation elevation" for water storage is limited to 1117 feet (340.5 m). Water above this level is discharged in order that appropriate "flood control" storage can be maintained. However, if water is released at a rate greater than 13,000 cubic feet per second (cfs) (368 cubic meters per second (cms)), it will result in the closing of some roads downstream (Bill Jeffers, IBWC, pers. comm., 1999).

- Under Article 5 of the 1944 treaty between the United States and Mexico, the two countries equally share power generation from Amistad Reservoir. There are two United States and two Mexican generators in the project, and electrical generation needs can be taken into account when planning the timing of releases. As it requires approximately three days for water released from Amistad Reservoir to reach Falcon Reservoir, some advanced planning is necessary to meet water deliveries from Falcon Reservoir and to efficiently meet desired electrical generation capabilities (Bill Jeffers, IBWC, pers. comm., 1999).

- At low water levels (such as are now being experienced) all downstream users may have their allocations cut back in equal proportions. However, municipal needs will generally receive a full allocation with agricultural allocations being more significantly reduced. Typically about 240,000 ac-ft (296 million cubic meters) of the United States allocation of water is used each year for domestic, municipal and industrial uses. Agricultural use will vary greatly dependent upon the amount of water available in Falcon/Amistad Reservoir storage system. When at "conservation elevation", approximately 85% of the water released from these dams (i.e. approximately 1.2 million ac-ft (1.48 billion cubic meters)) is available for agricultural uses. Severe drought conditions for the last seven years, however, has severely lowered the reservoirs, and in 1999 only 600,000 – 700,000 ac-ft (740 to 863 million cubic meters) of water were available for agricultural purposes (Carlos Rubinstein, TNRCC, pers. comm., 2000).

- There is an agreement that zero discharge does not occur from Amistad Dam for more than six consecutive hours, as this has potential adverse effects on domestic supply pumps further downstream (Bill Jeffers, IBWC, pers. comm., 1999).

Water Rights

Surface Water

Surface water rights are governed by the Texas Water Code and require either a permit issued by the Texas Natural Resources Conservation Commission, or a certificate of adjudication. Such water is broadly defined to include "the water of the ordinary flow, under flow, and tides of every flowing river, natural stream, and lake, and of every bay or arm of the Gulf of Mexico, and the stormwater, floodwater, and rainwater of every river, natural stream, canyon, ravine, depression, and watershed of the state"[6]. No water right is needed to capture storm water runoff. Permits are not required for small reservoirs (200 ac-ft (246.7 million cubic meters) or less) used for domestic or livestock purposes[7].

The discharge of a spring is considered to be surface water, and so is subject to appropriation pursuant to state statute. However, such water must have reached the surface of the ground in order to be considered surface water. Water that has not yet reached the surface of the ground presents another issue. If such water is still percolating through the soil, as opposed to flowing in a defined channel, a landowner may intercept such water and use it in accord with the rule of capture, as discussed below. If such water is flowing in a definite channel, it is considered to be surface water and so is subject to appropriation.[8]

Texas recognizes the traditional beneficial uses--industrial, municipal, irrigation--but also recognizes instream uses as well, including recreation, game preserves, stock raising, and park purposes[9].

As administrator of Amistad Reservoir, the IBWC releases water based on calls received from Mexico or the United States. In the case of a United States call for the Pecos River, water is released to the Pecos River master for distribution to United States water rights holders. The drainages of the Pecos and Devils Rivers are fully appropriated (Herman Settemyer, TNRCC, pers. comm., May, 2001). TNRCC records indicate that Amistad NRA holds no surface rights in the Pecos or Devils River drainages (Maria, TNRCC, Pecos Watermaster Office, pers. comm. May, 2001).

Ground Water

The State of Texas adheres to the "rule of capture" for ground water.[10] A landowner has the absolute right to pump as much water as he needs, but may not engage in intentional waste or malicious injury to adjacent landowners.[11] The definition of "beneficial use" is very broad, so that in essence, there is no restriction on the amounts or types of uses of ground water available to a landowner (Mike Chadwick, TNRCC, Ground Water Enforcement Team, May 2001). This approach has been shown to be ineffective as an allocation mechanism in the face of increasing water demand and continued drought, but it remains entrenched. Due to increasing demand for water the Texas legislature and

---

[6] R. E. Beck, 1991, ed., Waters and Water Rights 410, citing Tex. Water Code § 11.021.

[7] *Id.*, at 411.

[8] *Denis v. Kickapoo Land Co.*, 771 S.W.2d 235 (Civ.App., 3d Distr. 1989), citing *Texas Co. v. Burnett*, 296 S.W. 273 (Tex. 1927). See also Tex. Water Code Ann. § 52.002 (Supp.1989).

[9] Beck, *supra*, at 416.

[10] *Houston & T.C. Ry. v. East*, 81 S.W. 279 (Tex. 1904).

[11] *Id.*

judiciary have, in recent years, taken small steps away from the "rule of capture". The move away from this rule has been slow and incremental due to strong opposition from property rights advocates. Nevertheless, some commentators believe that regulation is inevitable, despite a history of strong protection of property rights by the Texas judiciary. At present, there is little regulation of ground water withdrawal with the exception of the Edwards Aquifer landowner (Mike Chadwick, TNRCC, Ground Water Enforcement Team, May 2001). The Edwards Aquifer Authority was created to protect and manage the aquifer. While portions of the aquifer extend under Amsitad NRA, the Authority's jurisdiction does not appear to encompass Amistad NRA.[12] As to areas outside the Authority's boundary, the only regulation of pumping or drilling for ground water would come from a local ground water management district (Roger Quincy, TNRCC, pers. comm., July, 2001).[13] A well completed into the alluvium or underflow of a river would need a surface water right, but a well completed into a deep aquifer is considered to be private property, and is subject only to the "rule of capture" as discussed above.

In order to best protect the NRA's present uses of ground water in the face of possible future regulation, Amistad NRA should document ground water use in order to ensure that the NRA's historical use is recognized and protected as a pre-regulation right.

Amsitad NRA Wells

Documentation maintained by the Water Resources Division indicates that Amistad NRA derives its water solely from underground sources. Overall, the documentation is sparse and does not support a good analysis or understanding of the water rights situation. A review of the NPS Water Rights Bureau dockets yielded the following information regarding the water resources at Amistad NRA.

- Rough Canyon Well:
    The Rough Canyon site is approximately 10 miles (16 km) upstream from the Amistad Dam on the Devils River. The docket contains a 1972 Memorandum from a Hydraulic Engineer from the Office of the Regional Chief Scientist. The Memorandum, prepared after a trip to the park, indicates that the well is expected to provide potable water for the park's present and future needs. A recent determination by park personnel indicates that the well is 520 feet (158 m) in depth. It is difficult to tell from the map how close the well site is to the river, but the well depth suggests that it is not in the alluvium. The NPS Water Resources Division files contain some documentation of pump tests and sparse record of water use.

- Diablo East Well:
    The Diablo East site is approximately 3 miles (4.8 km) upstream from the Amistad Dam, also on the Devils River. Information about this well is also available only from the 1972 Memorandum mentioned above, but that document provides little information about the well. The NPS Water Resources Division files contain some documentation of pump tests. A recent determination by park personnel indicates the well is completed to a depth of 490 feet (149 m).

A review of documents maintained by the NPR Water Resources Division contained information regarding other wells:

---

[12] Website, Edwards Aquifer Authority (www.edwardsaquifer.org), July 5, 2001.
[13] Several local government officers were contacted to determine if Val Verde County had a ground water management district, but none were aware that such a district existed.

- Pecos River Well:

    A NPS Water Resources Report (Christenson, 1981) indicates that the park also maintains a well in the Pecos River recreational site near the confluence of the Pecos and Rio Grande Rivers. The report discusses water quality but does not address any legal or water rights issues regarding the well. A recent determination by park personnel indicates the well is 625 feet (190 m) in depth.

- "480'" Well:

    There is sparse documentation of the so-called "480'" well, limited to water quality. The well is located approximately 1000 feet (305 m) north of intersection of Highway 90 and access road to dam. The well was drilled in 1964.

- Headquarters System:

    Sparse water quality data from 1979 is provided. A recent determination by park personnel indicates the well is 400 feet (122 m) in depth. No further information is available.

- Governor's Landing Well:

    Sparse water quality data provided for this well number 665-17. A recent determination by park personnel indicates the well is 390 feet (119 m) in depth. This well has also been referred to as the Devils River well.

Fisheries Management Plan

The Secretariat of Agriculture, Livestock, Rural Development, Fisheries, and Nutrition[14] (SAGARPA) in Mexico, along with the Texas Parks and Wildlife Department (TPWD), NPS, and the Fish and Wildlife Service (USFWS) in the United States, all have management responsibilities for various aspects of the aquatic resources within Amistad Reservoir and its surrounding drainages. All agencies concur that the communication among the agencies has not been adequate with regard to visitor services, management policies, implementation of harvest regulations, scientific research, and fish stocking.

In January 2000, the four agencies developed a proposal recommending the development of an international fisheries management plan (U.S. Dept. of Interior, 2000). In September 2000, representatives of TPWD, SEMARNAP, and the NPS conducted a meeting to both share information on current fishery management efforts and to establish goals and objectives for the development of an International Fisheries Management Plan.

At this meeting, participants agreed to an overall goal of completing an international fisheries management plan which will provide a framework for Mexican/United States fisheries resource managers to better manage the shared aquatic resources of Amistad Reservoir and the surrounding hydrologic basin. It is anticipated that an International Fisheries Management Plan will be completed by 2003.

---

[14] SEGARPA recently acquired the responsibility for managing Mexico's fishery resources after a reorganization of Mexican natural resource agencies in early 2001. Previously, fisheries were managed by the Secretariat of Environment, Natural Resources and Fisheries (SEMARNAP) which is now known as Secretariat of Environment, Natural Resources (SEMARNAT).

WATERSHED DESCRIPTION

Climate

The climate in the area of Amistad NRA is continental and semiarid. The humidity is generally low, especially during winter months, and greater rainfall potential exists from April through October each year. Precipitation averages between 17 to 18 inches (43 to 46 millimeters) annually, but there have been very dry years and severe drought conditions regionally for numerous years throughout much of Texas and portions of northern Mexico. Average low and high temperatures locally during the summer are 72 F and 97 F (22 C and 36 C), while 40 F and 64 F (4 C and 18 C) are average low and high temperatures experienced in the winter (NPS, 1987) (National Climate Data Center, 2000).

Geology

The land throughout most of southern Val Verde County is undulating to nearly level, but with steeper slopes and eroded canyon walls having ten to several hundred feet elevation differentials close to the rivers.

The subsurface geology surrounding Amistad NRA is one primarily of limestone in the Edwards Plateau. Several excellent papers and bulletins describe the stratigraphy, materials, setting, history, and presence of fossils and are briefly summarized below. Many geologic studies have been performed in the region for several reasons: easily accessible formation exposures in eroded river channels and road cuts; geotechnical studies for dam and petroleum studies; and the presence and great interest in large subsurface springs in this dry region.

The long stretch of US 90 north-northeast of the reservoir lies on a thick gray lower cretaceous limestone (the very same limestone that makes up the upper part of the cliffs in Santa Elena Canyon on the west side of Big Bend National Park). It is seen in numerous eroded and exposed locations in Amistad NRA including bluffs and cliffs west of the US 90 bridge over the reservoir and on the west side of the Pecos River canyon (US 90 bridge). The lower cretaceous limestones are overlain by upper cretaceous limestones nearby of the Austin chalk, Boquilas formation, the Buda limestone, and the Del Rio Clay in descending order. Numerous Buda limestone outcrop locations contain clam fossils (Spearing, 1991).

Excavations for the Amistad Dam construction and nearby drill cores gathered by the IBWC yielded detailed limestone bedrock definition. Nearly 450 feet (137 m) of the Salmon Peak Formation, consisting of lime mudstone overlays about 300 feet (91 meter) of limestone shales, anhydrite grainstones, and lime mudstones of the McKnight Formation (Smith et al, 1983).

The geologic history and hydrogeologic setting of the more than 42,000 square mile Edwards-Trinity aquifer system is described in a 1994 publication by the U.S. Geological Survey (USGS). Amistad NRA receives major groundwater flow through springs and partially spring-fed rivers that tap the Edwards-Trinity aquifer. Extensive fractures, joint cavities, and porosity caused by the dissolution of unstable carbonates and evaporites provide the conduit for the aquifer to Amistad Reservoir (Barker et al, 1994).

14

Soils

Soils along the United States side of Amistad Reservoir were derived from the parent limestone rock and formed through weathering and biological processes over thousands of years. The soils are almost entirely classified as Langtry-Rock outcrop Zorra. Most of these shallow, loamy soils are moderately alkaline, cobbly or stoney, about 8 inches deep, and usually found over fractured limestone bedrock or strongly cemented caliche; with exposed limestone outcrops commonly found on uplands (Golden et al, 1981). Suitability of these soils lies primarily for wildlife habitat or range, while urban and recreational uses are poor, because of depth to bedrock and slope considerations. None of the soils surrounding NRA or nearby are prime farmland soil types, but southeast of Amistad NRA and Del Rio some would be classified as such, but only if irrigation water was employed.

On the United States side of the Rio Grande, Amistad NRA lies within Val Verde County, Texas. On the Mexico side, the reservoir is located entirely within the state of Coahuila. The entire Val Verde county and State of Coahuila, in proximity to Amistad NRA, is rangeland for sheep, goats, and cattle (even with the increasing development of United States lands surrounding the reservoir for residential use). Rangeland use, while a suitable use of the soils types and vegetation surrounding Amistad Reservoir, can also be a cause of erosion, non-native plant/animal influx, and potential water quality impacts.

River Environments

Rio Grande

The Rio Grande along the Texas-Mexico border stretches nearly twelve hundred miles before reaching the Gulf of Mexico. More than 90% of the withdrawals of water from the Rio Grande are for irrigation, since there are substantial lands suitable for farming, that lack necessary water.

The Rio Grande section of the Amistad NRA begins 36 miles (58 km) above the confluence with the Pecos River. The park contains 6 miles (9.7 km) of flowing river between the NRA boundary at 1,144 feet (349 m) elevation and the reservoir water conservation pool of 1,117 feet (340 m). Since 1995, the Rio Grande has been free flowing beyond the Pecos River for a total of 40 river miles (64 km). The river forms a low gradient channel meandering within high canyon walls. The river has an adequate floodplain, however some portions of the channel are incised into silt deposits, due to the lack of regular high flows resulting from upstream dam regulation. Historically, the river channel was likely broad and shallow, winding through a floodplain populated with native willows and other riparian species.

The riparian zone along this section of the Rio Grande has become a complex woodland of native willow and huisache (*Acacia famesiana*) in places. However, other reaches of the river have vast expanses of exotic river cane and salt cedar (*Tamarix spp.*) (Figure 3). Many animals have returned to this habitat, including beaver which have benefited from the increase in willow growth.

Figure 3. Rio Grande River in Amistad NRA

Figure 4. Pecos River at Railroad Bridge

Pecos River

The Pecos River flows from the Southern Rocky Mountains in New Mexico through the oil producing Permian Basin in West Texas, south through spectacular limestone canyons to Amistad Reservoir, forming a large watershed of 44,000 square miles (11.4 million hectares). Water from the upper watershed has long been used for irrigation, and historical accounts document the change in the river from a broad wide river to a narrow sluggish stream after the onset of irrigation in 1877. Many parts of the river channel are now lined with salt cedar (*Tamarix spp.*), an exotic tree that transpires great amounts of water and adds salt to the streambanks where it grows.

Amistad NRA manages 16 miles (25.8 km) of the Pecos River. From the boundary to the reservoir conservation pool of 1,117 feet (340 m), the Pecos River flows for 3 miles (4.8 km). The Pecos River gauging station, near Langtry, is located at an elevation of 1,136 feet (346 m). Since 1995, the Pecos River has been free flowing for a total of 9 miles (14.9 km) from the boundary to Deadman's Canyon. Below Deadman's Canyon, the Pecos River is lined by steep limestone canyon walls and slows to a 6 mile (9.7 km) long pool to the US 90 bridge (Figure 4). Sediment deposition in the lower Pecos along with low reservoir water levels has formed the pool environment above the US 90 bridge. When the lake level is low, as at present, the Pecos flows from the US 90 bridge to the confluence with the Rio Grande for approximately one mile (1.6 km), forming a narrow shallow incised channel (Figure 5).

Figure 5. Pecos River just above Confluence with Rio Grande.

Since 1995, boaters have been unable to access the upper reaches of the Pecos River. The low water and high levels of sediment deposition have made boat travel very restrictive. The sediment deposits are covered with both salt cedar (*Tamarix spp.*), and native willow (*Salix sp.*) below the US 90 bridge. Between the bridge and Deadman's

Canyon, limestone canyon walls provide little habitat for salt cedar and willow development. Above Deadman's Canyon, salt cedar and willow are found in pockets where canyon walls widen to provide riparian habitats.

Figure 6. Aerial Close up of Devils River Channel

Figure 7. Devils River above Amistad Reservoir

Devils River

The Devils River drains an area of 4,305 square miles (1.1 million hectares). This spring fed river is not regulated and is under very little influence by land use in the watershed, which is primarily ranches and small rural housing developments.

Amistad NRA manages 2.7 flowing river miles (4.3 km) on the Devils River when water levels are at the reservoir conservation pool. Since 1995, the Devils River has flowed for an additional 4.3 miles (6.9 km) due to low reservoir levels. This has resulted in a total of 7 miles (11.3 km) of free flowing river from the boundary to approximately 1 mile (1.6 km) below Satan Canyon. The Pafford Crossing gauging station on the Devils River is found at an elevation of 1,134 feet (346 m), and is 1.1 miles (1.8 km) below the NRA boundary.

The Devils River flows over a base structure of limestone shelves, forming swift narrow runs alternating with calm braided channels and slow flowing pools (Figure 6). Pecan, oak and sycamore are found along the riverbanks (Figure 7). Salt cedar has not become a nuisance exotic species in this system, due to the semi-annual high flows, which scour shorelines and benefit native plant regeneration.

Vegetation and Shoreline environment

Adjacent Land Use

Historically, ranching was the primary land use in the Amistad Reservoir area. Prior to the establishment of Amistad Reservoir, sheep, goat and cattle ranches were located along the Rio Grande, Devils and Pecos Rivers. Ranching continues today on the uplands adjacent to the recreation area boundary. Grazing is allowed within the recreation area by permit (see Effects of Grazing Section). Recent population growth has resulted in several new small subdivisions scattered around the reservoir shoreline, mostly to provide retirement and vacation housing.

Upland Vegetation Communities

Vegetation found at Amistad NRA is represented by the Chihuahuan desert, Edwards plateau, and the Tamaulipan scrub biotic regions. These three regions converge in southwest Texas to form a number of plant communities. Three series-level plant communities, as outlined by the Texas Natural Heritage Program (TNHP) (1993) have been identified for Amistad NRA. These include three shrublands, the Cenizo Series, Guajillo Series, and Blackbrush Series, which all tend to intergrade. For general description, the vegetation at Amistad could be assigned to the Blackbrush Series (TNHP, 1995). Guajillo (*Acacia berlandieri*) and cenizo (*Leucophyllum frutescens*) are common plants throughout much of the park, but blackbrush (*Acacia rigidula*) is probably the dominant species (TNHP, 1995). A highly disturbed plant community unassignable to series level occurs in the zone of the fluctuating lake level.

The Blackbrush Series occupies more or less level plateau tops and is found on gentle to steep slopes along drainages, primarily over shallow soils. This series, in the NRA, ranges in elevation from 1,117 feet (340 m) to 1,144 feet (349 m). Percent cover is variable, depending on the amount of limestone bedrock exposed and the topography. Cover on relatively flat plateaus and slopes leading to drainages ranges from 25 to 50 percent (TNHP, 1995). In addition to blackbrush, cenizo, and guajillo, other common woody species include Texas persimmon (*Diospyros texana*), coyotillo (*Karwinskia humboldtiana*), and border pricklypear (*Opuntia atrispina*) (TNHP, 1995).

Riparian Plant Communities

A list of herbaceous plants has been prepared for Amistad (TNHP, 1995), but it only includes plants found in close proximity to the reservoir itself and the source rivers. Plant life has not been extensively studied in the riparian and aquatic portions of the reservoir, mainly due to the highly fluctuating water level throughout seasons and years and the NRA's legislated purpose to manage recreational use rather than scientific research.

There are photographic and some written records of riparian vegetation nearly a century ago, that include a sparse and somewhat dynamic community of cottonwoods and willows on bars and banks of the three rivers. Similar, but somewhat more stable plant groupings would have been found in the many spring fed small drainages, joining the rivers. Some of these side drainages that exist above the reservoir's conservation level probably look similar to their historic past, albeit recently modified by non-native plants and livestock grazing.

Due to fluctuating water levels in Amistad Reservoir, a shoreline disturbed zone supporting more mesic-adapted, weedy species has developed. The width of this zone varies with topography and lake level fluctuations. Percent cover depends on the amount of time the limestone rock or silt in the drowned canyons is exposed. Recently uncovered areas and frequently flooded zones are usually devoid of vegetation while areas which have been exposed for several months or years may support a 10 to 75 percent cover of such invasive, non-native species as salt cedar (*Tamarix sp.*) and tree *tobacco (Nicotiana glauca)*. Roosevelt weed (*Baccharis neglecta*) is an abundant native species in this area (TNHP, 1995).

Where water levels in the reservoir have remained relatively constant for several years, extensive colonization occurs along the water's edge and in shallow embayments by some of the rush, bulrush and sedge communities as well as some purely aquatic species (e.g. Potamogeton *sp.*). Even the cottonwood and willow seedlings will start in moist areas, but are frequently short-lived because of inundation or exposure and desiccation from water level fluctuations.

Riparian plant communities have altered due to the creation and operation of the dam as well as from the introduction of non-native species. This change in plant communities may cause long term impacts to the NRA's purpose, reservoir operations, and health of the ecosystem. Extensive portions of the Rio Grande and portions of the Pecos River, where suitable gravel or silt beds are exposed or have shallow, slow moving water over them are densely covered with exotics such as river cane (*Arundo sp.*) and salt cedar (*Tamarix spp.*), as well as native species of willow (*Salix sp*), and huisache (*Acacia famesiana*). In lower reaches of the rivers and reservoir where broad and flat-sloped shorelines are exposed close to neighboring grazing areas, large communities of non-native grasses and herbaceous plants abound. Where limestone rocky slopes occur in the reservoir, non-native tree tobacco (*Nicotiana glauca*) dominates. Salt cedar and river cane form nearly impenetrable barriers along the riverbanks, making it difficult to access riparian areas from the water. During periods of rising water levels or floods, mats of dead river cane can form, creating barriers to navigation on the river and in the reservoir. Dead plant material adds to the already high sedimentation rate in the upper reaches of the reservoir that will continue to affect the channel morphology for visitor use. Floating plant material and non-native seeds may also ultimately affect other areas of the reservoir shore for visitors and possibly the operation of the dam for irrigation and hydropower purposes.

Groundwater

Surrounding the reservoir, water levels in ground-water wells developed in the McKnight and associated limestones increased significantly (by up to 100 feet (30.5 m)) after the filling of the reservoir (Reeves and Small 1973). While water from Amistad Reservoir has been identified extensively in McKnight and associated limestone groundwater wells throughout Val Verde County, no Amistad Reservoir water was found in a recent analysis of San Felipe Springs. The author of that same analysis concluded that 85% of groundwater near the reservoir came from the reservoir, while at approximately eight miles from the reservoir, groundwater was only 30% reservoir water (Armstrong 1995). The author performed his study during a period of relative high water levels in the reservoir; thus his conclusions should be cautiously interpreted for more recent low water conditions at Amistad Reservoir.

Prior to the construction of the reservoir, regional groundwater movements from the United States were southwesterly, and northeasterly in Mexico, both towards the Rio Grande. Under partial and full conditions of the reservoir, groundwater flow proceeds more southerly in the United States, while in Mexico the flow is believed to move east-southeasterly (Reeves and Small 1973).

Groundwater Quality

The 1995 study by Armstrong that documented movement of Amistad Reservoir water into springs and wells under high reservoir level conditions reached several conclusions for groundwater quality.

- A portion of surface water in Amistad Reservoir and groundwater in the McKnight and associated limestones originate from the same source.

- The McKnight and associated limestones surrounding Amistad Reservoir are susceptible to contamination from waters in Amistad Reservoir.

- Recharge of the regional groundwater flow system occurs in the Devils River drainage basin and outcrops of the McKnight and associated limestones.

- Between the Amistad Reservoir Dam and the international bridge at Ciudad Acuna, the Rio Grande loses water to the alluvial and terrace deposits in the river valley.

- The McKnight and associated limestones regionally are not significantly threatened by water lost by the Rio Grande.

Springs and Seeps

Springs, the discharge of groundwater at the surface, have been very important to inhabitants of the border area between Texas and Mexico. The springs' significance precedes even the arrival of the first humans in the area, as formative agents of hydrogeological processes and important factors for vegetative and wildlife habitat developments. Early human discoveries of springs in more arid regions or dry seasons would have established potable water sources. They also would have laid the patterns for

21

early hunting sites, trails for communication and commerce, settlements, and some agriculture by irrigation.

In a study published in 1975, Texas was found to originally have had more than 280 major and historically significant springs, with more than half of those significantly decreased in flow or having ceased to flow entirely. More than half of the significant springs were found to emanate from the Edwards and the Edwards-Trinity Aquifers, with the larger springs in the Amistad NRA originating from the latter. Known springs at the Amistad NRA and the large San Felipe spring in Del Rio flow from the Georgetown Formation Limestones of the Edwards-Trinity Aquifer (Brune 1975). The Georgetown Formation Limestones, known locally as the McKnight and associated limestones, actively transmit much of the ground water and spring water to the south-southwest in Val Verde County (Armstrong 1995). Major springs of Amistad NRA are described in Table 2.

Figure 8. Indian Springs

Historical Spring Flow

Historically, springs such as San Felipe Spring, Goodenough Spring, and many others throughout the state, flowed under large amounts of pressure and produced fountains at the surface. Pressure release due to well drilling, and head decrease due to long years of

22

pumping for drinking supply and agricultural use have reduced the flows significantly at these and many other springs. Some spring flow may also have decreased due to reduced recharge over the watershed due to a shift from grass to shrub cover, and the resulting loss of infiltration capacity, resulting from grazing over the past 100 years. The completion of the Amistad Reservoir in 1969 covered many springs in the area and increased the flow of others downstream. The Cantu or Cienaga Spring, located just downstream of the Amistad Reservoir dam on the Rio Grande also has had an increased flow since the reservoir construction.

Existing Springs of Amistad NRA

Devils River Watershed

The Devils River has one of the largest base flows of Texas rivers due to spring flow (Brune, 1981), and a few springs, such as Willow Springs and Indian Springs are still visible depending on water level (Figure 8). Historic springs noted in the Devils River watershed include: Juno, Headwater, or Stein Springs (originally two springs; dry in 1971, Pecan Springs (originally 6 springs; only one flowing in 1971), Hudspeth Springs (many springs; still flowing in 1971), Finegan Springs (originally 25 springs; nine remain flowing in 1971), Dolan Springs (two main and 20 smaller springs continue flowing in 1971), Gillis Springs (about 14 springs, some below river level, still flowing in 1971).

Table 2. Major Springs within Amistad NRA.

Spring Name	Location	Elevation	Spring Flow
Devils River			
Willow Springs	Along Devils River	Slightly above conservation pool	4121 gpm (260 lps) (1971)
Indian Springs	Limestone bluff on east shore of lake	At conservation pool	Range: 4913 gpm (310 lps) (1971) to 20,605 gpm (1,300 lps) (1925)
Satan Springs	Mouth of Satan Creek	At conservation pool	54 gpm (3.4 lps)
Lester Springs	2 miles (3.2 km) south of Indian Springs	Inundated	90 gpm (5.7 lps)
Rio Grande			
Goodenough Springs	Along Rio Grande	Inundated	61,818 gpm (3,900 lps) (average annual flow)
Pump Canyon Springs	1.5 (2.4 km) miles west of Langtry	At conservation pool	135 gpm (8.5 lps) (1939)
Eagle Nest Springs	Upper reach of Rio Grande	Inundated	4.9 gpm (0.31 lps) (1968)
Pecos River			
Dead Man Springs	East side of River, north of railroad	56 feet (17 m) below conservation pool	1902 gpm (120 lps) (1939)
Pecos Springs	2.5 miles (4.0 km) south of Dead Man Springs	Inundated	25.5 gpm (1.61 lps) (1939)

Summarized from Brune, 1981.

Satan springs, at the mouth of Satan Creek, issues from several openings in limestone precisely at the conservation pool level of Amistad Reservoir (Brune, 1981). At low reservoir water levels, this spring flows for approximately 0.5 miles (0.8 kilometer), before reaching the Devils River. This area provides an example of the wetlands that develop when reservoir water levels are low. Cattails and many species of sedges can be found growing along this water flow. Many unnamed small springs have been observed around the reservoir during low reservoir water levels.

Pecos River Watershed

The Pecos River also has several named springs within Amistad NRA. Dead Man Springs and Pecos Springs in the Pecos drainage are both inundated at conservation pool. Dead Man Springs can be found on the east side of the river, north of the Southern Pacific railroad, inundated under about 56 feet (17 m) of water when the reservoir is at conservation pool level (Brune, 1981). With the recent low lake levels, these springs have been above the water level since 1994. Several small springs were identified in the Pecos River above the Amistad NRA boundary: Howard Springs and Tardy Springs (nine springs) and Cox Springs (23 springs).

Rio Grande Watershed

Along the Rio Grande River within Amistad NRA, the very large and significant artesian Goodenough Spring flows into the reservoir below surface, in all but the driest of years. On July 11, 1968, Amistad Reservoir flooded Goodenough Springs. This was the third largest spring in Texas (Brune, 1981). They are now under 151 feet (46 m) of water when the reservoir is at conservation pool level. In November 1999, when Goodenough Spring was approximately ten meters beneath the reservoir surface, the reservoir surface was visibly roiled by the discharge (John Reber, NPS Water Resources Division, site visit 11/99).

Two km west of Langtry on the Rio Grande is Pump Canyon springs on the Rio Grande, which flows into the lake both above and below conservation pool level. Eagle Nest Springs is a group of springs which flows into the upper reaches of the Rio Grande within Amistad NRA. Only one other spring along the Rio Grande (McKee Springs), upstream of the reservoir, was identified in the 1975 Brune study. Its flow has increased since the reservoir construction in 1968.

WATER FLOWS

Introduction

Flow from the Rio Grande (Rio Bravo), Pecos River and the Devils River; account for more than 70% of the estimated inflows to Amistad Reservoir. The remaining third of reservoir inflows are contributed primarily from springs, the largest being Goodenough Spring, which was inundated when the reservoir filled. Early streamflow records show that Goodenough Spring averaged almost 62,000 cubic feet per second (cfs) (1,750 cubic meters per second (cms)). Other springs are located along the Devils River below the gauging station and around the circumference of the reservoir as described in the previous section. In response to localized rainstorms, several ungauged Mexican arroyos also flow into the reservoir.

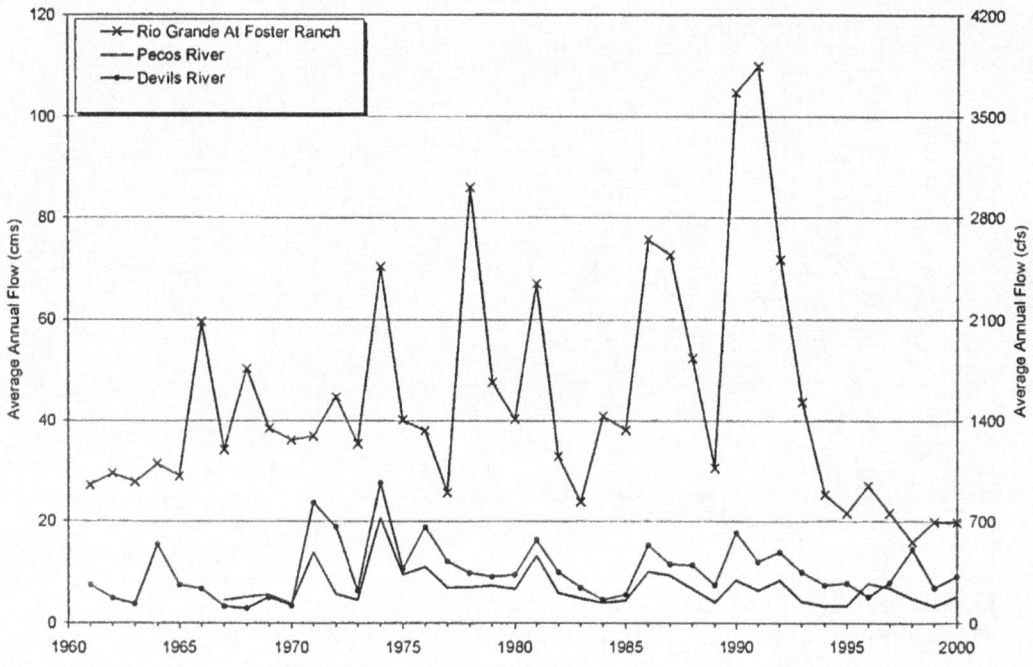

Figure 1. Annual Mean Flow of the Major Tributaries to Amistad Reservoir.

The Rio Grande provides the majority of flow to the reservoir, although over the past several years inflow of the Rio Grande has dropped to it's lowest recorded level since the construction of the reservoir (Figure 9).

USGS and IBWC gauging stations are located on all three major tributaries near their inflow into the reservoir. All streamflow data for this report and was obtained from the IBWC website (www.ibwc.state.gov/), and is given in both metric (cubic meters per second) and english (cubic feet per second) units in this report.

25

Rio Grande above Amistad

Two rivers come together to form the Rio Grande above Amistad NRA. The Upper Rio Grande originates from the Rocky Mountains in Colorado and New Mexico and the Rio Conchos flows from the Sierra Madres of Western Chihuahua, Mexico. The two rivers join at Ojinaga, Chihuahua and Presidio, Texas, about 60 miles (97 km) upstream from Big Bend National Park. The flow from these rivers accounts for over two-thirds of Rio Grande flow entering Amistad Reservoir. Until 1993, the majority of the flow into the reservoir from the Rio Grande came from the Rio Conchos (Figure 10). However, below average precipitation and increased water use in the Rio Conchos Basin have decreased the flow from this river. Other sources of water into the Rio Grande include many springs along the limestone canyons above the reservoir and the arroyos, which flow in response to rainstorms along this isolated stretch of the Rio Grande.

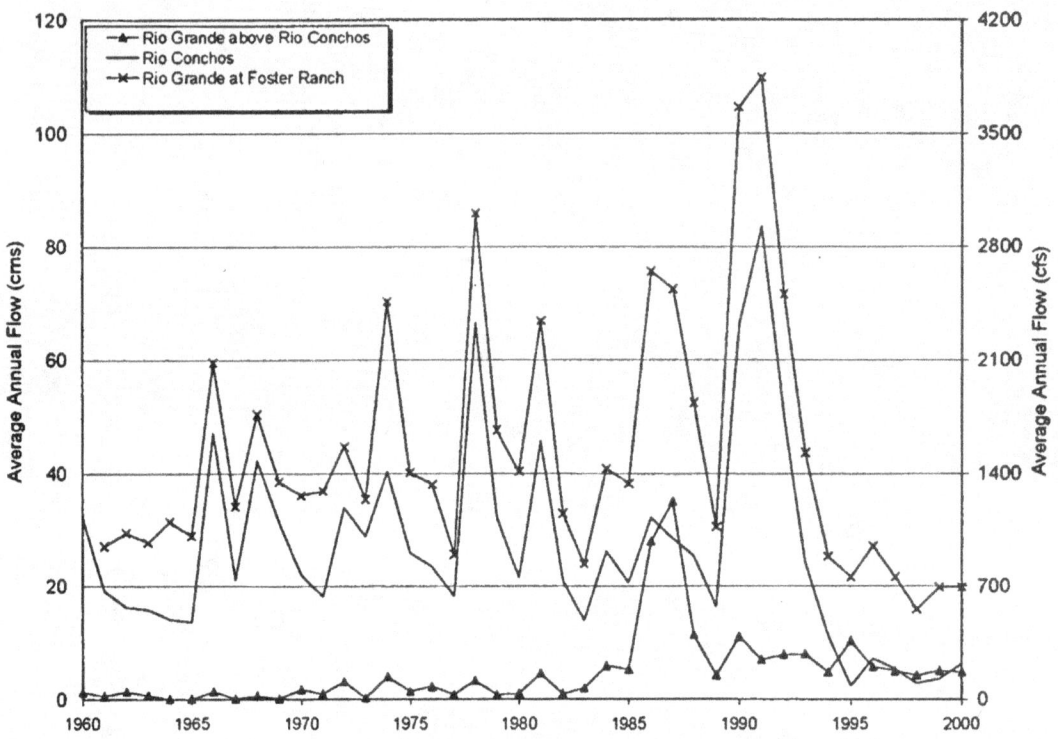

Figure 10. Average annual flows of the Rio Conchos, Rio Grande above the Rio Conchos and Rio Grande at Foster Ranch (just above Amistad Reservoir).

The Rio Grande in New Mexico and Colorado has numerous dams capable of holding several years of runoff, allowing storage during high flow years to supplement dry years and virtually eliminating floods, even during high snowpack years. Diversions for irrigation and municipalities leave sections of the Rio Grande dry in central New Mexico. The Rio Conchos is much less developed, with smaller dams, however, both population and agriculture are projected to continue growing (Kelly, 2001). Increased growth in the Rio Conchos Basin could result in continued reduction in flows to the Rio Grande, especially during dry years.

Prior to dams on the upper Rio Grande, the Rio Grande above Amistad would often have high flows in both May-June and in September, with the largest flows always from the Rio

Conchos in September (Schmidt and Everett, 2000). Currently, the high flow months for this part of the Rio Grande are September and October, when the Rio Conchos Basin receives rainfall from the summer monsoonal storm pattern.

Dams and water use by cities and for irrigation have reduced average high flows for both rivers. For the Rio Grande above the Rio Conchos, annual floods have been reduced to less than 25% of their original flow. The floods in the river below the Rio Conchos have been reduced by approximately 50% from the pre-dam era (Schmidt and Everett, 2000).

The contribution of flow from the Rio Conchos has decreased over the past seven years. As a result, in addition to reducing the total volume of flow, the proportion of flow from the Upper Rio Grande has correspondingly increased, except during the rainy season. Since 1960, the average contribution of the Rio Conchos was 80% of the total flow in the Rio Grande above Amistad, compared to only 57% since 1993.

The quality of water in the Rio Grande flowing into Amistad Reservoir has degraded over the last eight years, due to the decreased flows from the Rio Conchos and the elevated salinity levels in the Rio Grande above the Rio Conchos. See the Issues Section for more discussion of these trends.

Pecos River

The upper Pecos River has several reservoirs and irrigation diversions before it flows through the limestone canyons of the Edwards Trinity Plateau into Amistad Reservoir. Several small reservoirs impound water for irrigation along the Pecos River in Texas, in addition to the larger Red Bluff Reservoir (307,000 acre-feet) at the Texas - New Mexico state line. This reservoir was completed in 1936 for irrigation and power generation.

Peak flows can occur both in late spring due to snowmelt runoff from the upper watershed as well as during the summer monsoon season (Figure 11). Peak flows from spring runoff are reduced as Red Bluff Reservoir captures much of this water. Streamflow records for the lower Pecos are only available since 1968. For this period of record, the highest recorded daily peak flow was 29,416 cfs (833 cms) on September 22, 1974, although peak flows generally range between 1765 cfs (50 cms) and 14,125 cfs (400 cms). Peak flows do not appear to have been reduced over the past 40 years, probably because the impoundments on the Pecos River in Texas are relatively small.

However, total annual flow has declined steadily since the 1970's (Figure 9) and baseflow, ranging from 71 to 177 cfs (2 to 5 cms), has become lower and more prolonged, due to the increasing surface and groundwater use in the Permian Basin and in New Mexico.

Devils River

The Devils River is a spring fed river arising from the limestone formation known as the Edwards Plateau. Peak flows are highly dependent upon rainstorms, and flow can increase quickly from 70 cfs (2 cms) to over 3531 cfs (100 cms), in response to a large rainstorm. Streamflow records date from 1960 for the USGS gauging station at Pafford Crossing near Comstock, just above Amistad Reservoir (Figure 16). This portion of the Edwards Plateau is scarcely populated, but the increasing suburban development in the areas surrounding Austin and San Antonio may eventually increase population in this watershed.

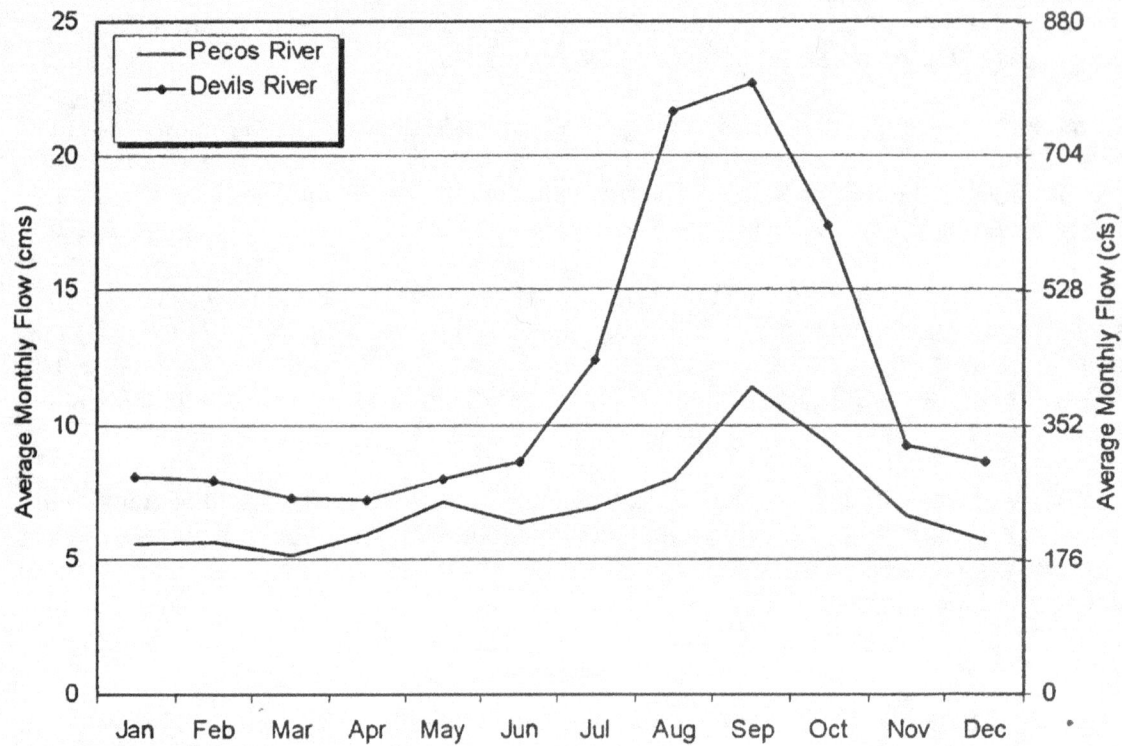

Figure 11. Average Monthly Flow of Pecos and Devils Rivers (1968-1999).

Base flows, originating from springs, average from 106 to 247 cfs (3 to 7 cms). Unlike the other inflows to Amistad Reservoir, base flows appear to be steady over the past 40 years. However, flows could decrease if groundwater use increases in this watershed.

Peak flows occur most often from August to October in response to rainstorms during the summer monsoon season. Extreme high flows occur as a result of hurricanes, most often during September or October. Flows over 35,314 cfs (1000 cms) have occurred 19 times since 1960. The highest recorded flow was 122,893 cfs (3480 cms) on September 18, 1974.

Peak flows are very flashy, with a typical high flow often lasting only a few days. In 1998, a tropical storm stalled over the Del Rio area resulted in a peak flow of 83,341 cfs (2360 cms). In addition, the river had higher base flows for close to a year following the storm (Figure 12). Large storms apparently recharge the limestone aquifer in the watershed, producing higher spring and groundwater flow to the Devils River for months and possibly years after a large rain event.

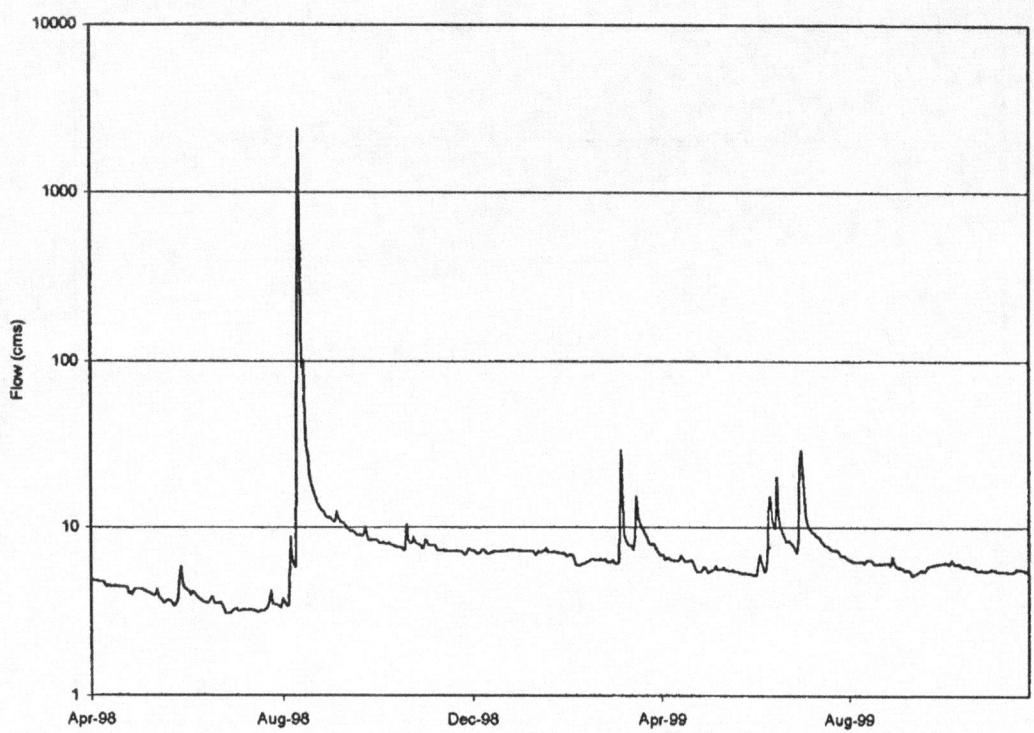

Figure 12. Increase in Devils River Base Flow Following a Large Rain Event in September, 1998.

Amistad Reservoir

After Amistad Dam was completed in 1969, several high flow years in the early 1970's quickly filled the reservoir, and may have deposited more sediment than anticipated. Lake level has always fluctuated, principally depending upon the inflows from the Rio Grande. However, since 1994, lake level has remained below 1085 feet (331 m), which is 32 feet (10 m) below the conservation pool elevation (Figure 13).

Water level fluctuations in the reservoir are usually less than 0.7 feet (0.2 m) per day. However, during irrigation season in the spring, the reservoir can be drawn down several meters or more. During the Spring of 1998, the reservoir was drawn down over 23 feet (7 m) between April and July. Tropical storms can also cause the reservoir to rise over 10 feet (several meters) in one day, as occurred in August 1998.

Reservoir Siltation Rate

When Amistad Reservoir was designed, the expected siltation rate was 10,700 acre-feet (13.19 million cubic meters) per year. The last siltation survey was completed in 1993, and estimated that the current siltation rate is 14,000 acre-feet (17.27 million cubic meters) per year (Ken Rakestraw, IBWC pers. comm. 11/3/2000). Most of the silt is deposited in the upper reaches of the reservoir in the Rio Grande arm and Pecos River arms of the reservoir. The siltation in these areas is causing access problems for the NRA, which are discussed in detail below in the Issues Section.

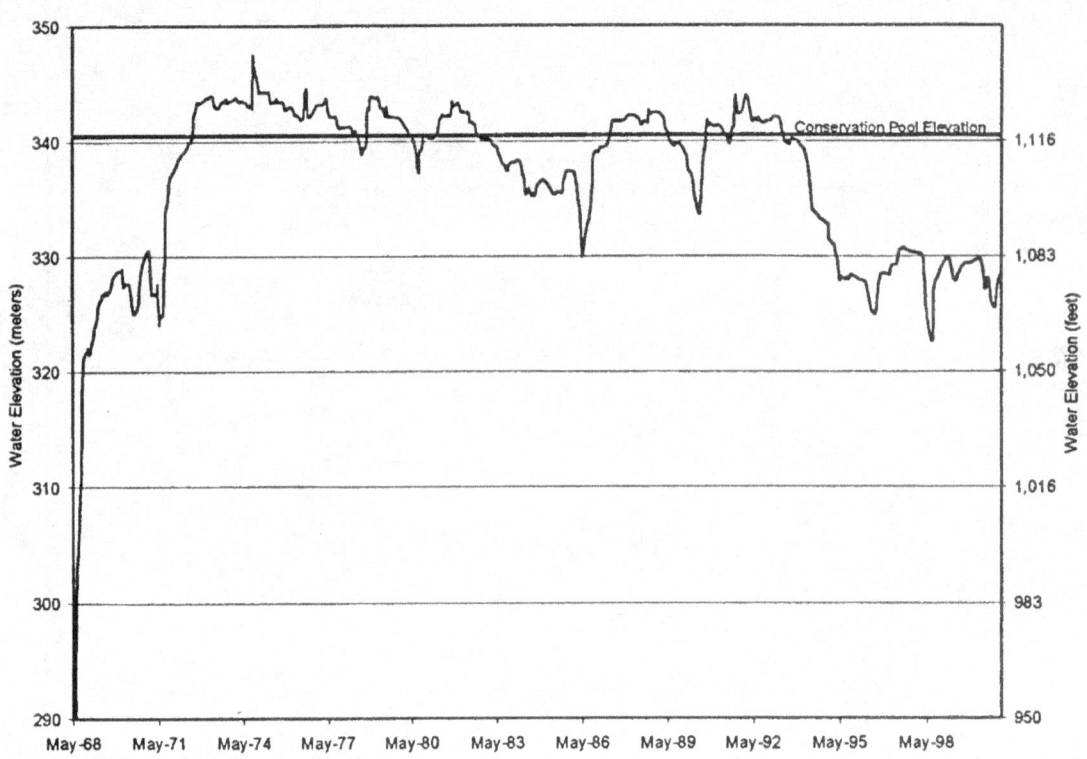

Figure 13. Water Level Elevation of Amistad Reservoir.

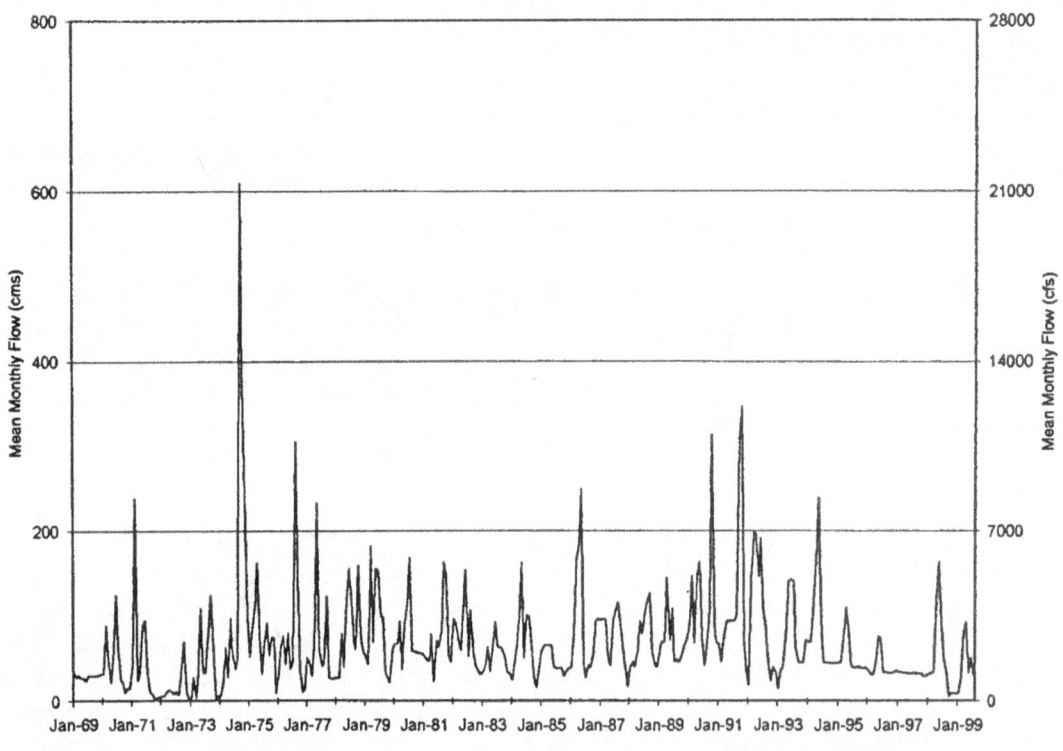

Figure 14. Average Monthly Ouflow from Amistad Dam (in cms) from 1969 to Present

Rio Grande Below Amistad

Outflows through Amistad dam typically are highest during the irrigation season from spring through early summer. The largest flood since the reservoir was completed occurred in September 1974. Several other smaller floods occurred in the late 1970's and the early 1990's (Figure 14). A 1998 tropical storm caused flooding in San Felipe Creek, which flows, into the Rio Grande near the town of Del Rio. Reservoir releases have decreased significantly since 1994 due to the decreased flow from the Rio Grande. Figure 15 illustrates the abruptness of the water releases. This unnatural hydrograph is undoubtedly affecting the riparian area directly below Amistad Dam. The abrupt increase and decrease of flow will tend to inhibit the formation and maintenance of channel point bars and riparian areas, and so decreases the aquatic and riparian habitat in this section of the Rio Grande.

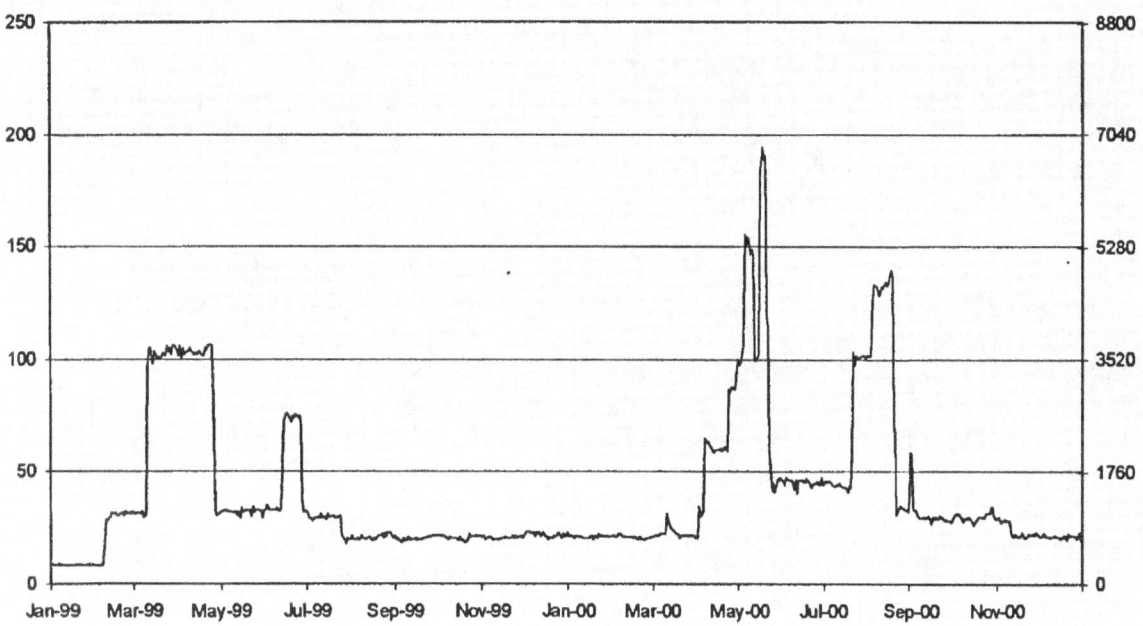

Figure 15. **Average daily Amistad Dam Outflows (in cms) for 1990 through 1999.**

WATER QUALITY

Introduction

Water quality in the Rio Grande has been the subject of many studies and monitoring efforts by several agencies. A long enough period of record exists to be able to detect trends, particularly the rising salinity and increases in several trace metals. Pecos River water quality has also been fairly well studied. The Devils River has less information available, although the existing data indicates the water quality is excellent with a low risk of future contamination.

Current Water Quality Monitoring Programs

Both the Texas Natural Resources Commission (TNRCC) and the U.S. Geological Survey (USGS) have active water quality monitoring programs in and around Amistad Reservoir. Figure 16 gives the locations of these monitoring sites. Both agencies sample the major tributaries to the reservoir; the Pecos, Devils and Rio Grande rivers, as well as the Rio Grande below the dam. TNRCC also samples the reservoir at three locations for field parameters, nutrients, chlorophyll and bacteria. Table 3 lists the constituents and sampling frequency for these sites.

The USGS sites on the Pecos River near Langtry, and Rio Grande at Foster Ranch have been part of the Rio Grande NASQAN (National Stream Quality Accounting Network) monitoring program since 1996. The Rio Grande 3.4 miles (5.5 km) below Amistad Dam station has been part of the NASQAN program since 1997. These sites are sampled 6 to 8 times a year for a variety of constituents, including nutrients, major ions, water soluble pesticides and trace elements. The Rio Grande NASQAN Program for 2001 - 2005 will continue to monitor these sites (Lurry, 2000). The Devils River at Pafford Crossing near Comstock, TX site is a recently discontinued USGS hydrologic benchmark station. This station was sampled four times a year for major nutrients, major ions and trace elements. This station is currently sampled by TNRCC Surface Water Quality Monitoring Program (SWQM) staff; the flow gauge is now operated by the IBWC.

Monitoring sites that are part of TNRCC's SWQM Program are funded by the U.S. Environmental Protection Agency (USEPA) grant money. TNRCC and USGS have collected water quality data at most of these stations since the 1970's, although the parameters collected and sampling frequency have varied. These stations have been sampled for the parameters listed in Table 3 since 1997.

Through the Texas Clean Rivers Program (CRP) funds, the IBWC coordinates monitoring activities in the Rio Grande Basin by supporting efforts of monitoring partners including: IBWC, TNRCC, USGS, NPS, Upper Pecos Soil and Water Conservation District, Cities of Del Rio, Laredo and Brownsville and the Rio Grande International Study Center at Laredo. This program supports special projects, acts as a clearing house for data (except for TNRCC and USGS data), provides a point of contact for issues in the Rio Grande Basin and provides annual summary reports. These activities are generally carried out by river authorities in other parts of Texas. As a part of the CRP, IBWC funds lab analysis and shipping costs for water quality samples collected upstream in Big Bend National Park.

Each year the IBWC Texas CRP staff coordinate meetings with monitoring partners to generate a coordinated monitoring schedule for the Rio Grande Basin. This effort allows for better monitoring coverage, reduces duplicate monitoring activities and supplements existing monitoring programs of TNRCC, USGS and IBWC. Information on this program can be found on the Rio Grande CRP website: www.ibwc.state.gov/crp/welcome.htm.

Planned and Ongoing Water Quality Studies

Two special studies are planned as part of the USGS Rio Grande NASQAN Program for 2001-2005 (Lurry, 2000). One study will determine seasonal patterns in thermal and density stratification in the Amistad and Falcon Reservoirs with additional monitoring for mercury deposition. This study will sample water quality at different depths and locations around the reservoir to determine the thermal and salinity characteristics.

Another study will collect continuous conductivity measurements to better understand salt flux in the Pecos River, Rio Grande at Foster's Ranch and Rio Grande at Presidio. This will provide additional information needed to estimate salt loading into Amistad Reservoir.

TNRCC is developing biocriteria for the Rio Grande between El Paso and Brownsville as part of a USEPA funded project. This project is scheduled for completion in 2002. In an effort to make these biocriteria binational, a working group with Mexico is being planned for winter of 2002.

A joint TNRCC and Texas Department of Health project collected fish for consumption risk in the Rio Grande between Presidio and Amistad Reservoir in April 2001. Fish collection occurred downstream of Presidio, TX and in Big Bend National Park.

Currently, there is an on-going USGS study of aquatic life and riparian areas covering the Rio Grande from Big Bend National Park downstream to Foster's Ranch. This study will develop baseline conditions for aquatic life and help examine the effects of prolonged low flows. The study is being conducted by Dr. Bruce Moring of the USGS Texas District (Austin) and is being partially funded by NPS-USGS partnership funds.

The USGS, NPS, TNRCC and IBWC are currently working together to design and seek funding for a study of metals in the Rio Grande above Amistad. This mulit-year study would analyze the amount of metals and other contaminants from historical mining which reach the Rio Grande in the Big Bend area.

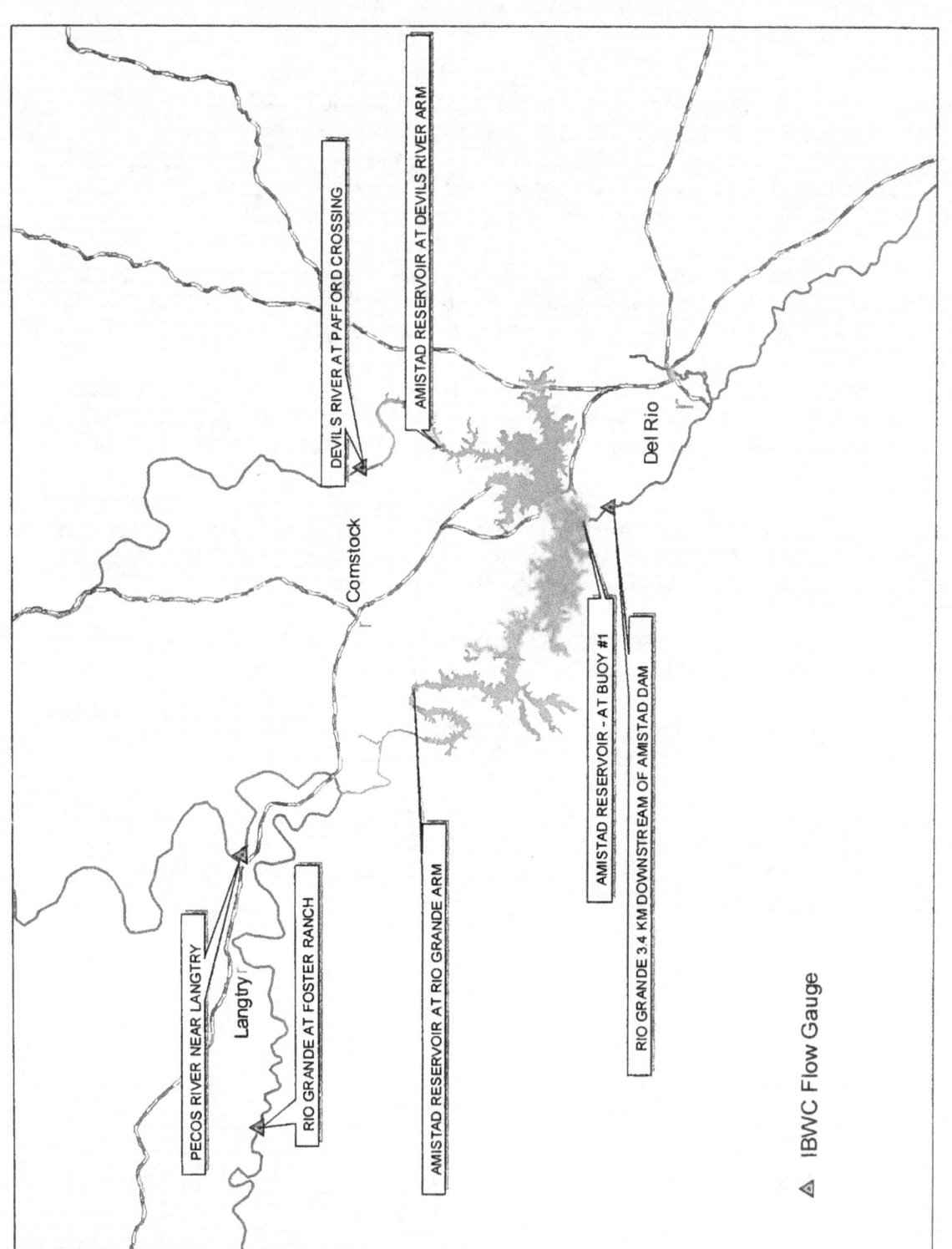

PECOS RIVER NEAR LANGTRY

RIO GRANDE AT FOSTER RANCH

AMISTAD RESERVOIR AT RIO GRANDE ARM

AMISTAD RESERVOIR - AT BUOY #1

RIO GRANDE 3.4 KM DOWNSTREAM OF AMISTAD DAM

DEVILS RIVER AT PAFFORD CROSSING

AMISTAD RESERVOIR AT DEVILS RIVER ARM

Langtry

Comstock

Del Rio

△ IBWC Flow Gauge

Figure 16. Map of Water Quality and Stream Flow Gauging Stations in the Amistad Area.

34

Table 3. Active Water Quality Monitoring Stations

Station Name	Agency	Station ID	# Samples per year	Parameters[15]
Rio Grande at Foster Ranch near Langtry*	USGS	8377200	8	Field Parameters, Nutrients, Major Ions, Trace Elements, Dissolved Pesticides
	TNRCC	13223	2	Field Parameters, Metals, Chloride, Sulfate, Nutrients, Bacteria, Chlorophyll a
Pecos River at Gauging Station at Langtry *	USGS	8447410	8	Field Parameters, Nutrients, Major Ions, Trace Elements, Dissolved Pesticides
	TNRCC	13240	2	Field Parameters, Metals, Nutrients, Chloride, Sulfate, Bacteria, Chlorophyll a
Devils River at Pafford Crossing near Comstock *	TNRCC	13237	4	Field Parameters, Nutrients, Chloride, Sulfate, Bacteria, Chlorophyll a
Rio Grande 3.4 km downstream of Amistad Dam, (above weir dam) *	USGS	8450900	6	Field Parameters, Nutrients, Major Ions, Trace Elements, Dissolved Pesticides
	TNRCC	15340	2	Field Parameters, Nutrients, Chloride, Sulfate, Bacteria, Chlorophyll a
Amistad Reservoir - Devils River Arm at Buoy DRP	TNRCC	15893	4	Field Parameters, Nutrients, Chloride, Sulfate, Bacteria, Chlorophyll a
Amistad Reservoir - Rio Grande Arm at Buoy 28	TNRCC	15892	4	Field Parameters, Nutrients, Chloride, Sulfate, Bacteria, Chlorophyll a
Amistad Reservoir - at Buoy #1	TNRCC	13835	4	Field Parameters, Nutrients, Chloride, Sulfate, Bacteria, Chlorophyll a

From 2001 Texas Clean Rivers Program Schedule and USGS NASQAN website (http://water.usgs.gov/nasqan).
* Gauging Station

---

[15] Field Parameters include Temp, Turbidity, Conductance, D.O., pH, CO_3, HCO^3, Alkalinity, % fines, and Suspended Sediment (TSS), TDS.
Nutrients include: Organic Carbon, Ammonia, Nitrite+Nitrate, Orthophosphorus and Total Phosphorus
Major Ions include: Chloride, Sulfate, Calcium, Sodium, and Potassium.
Trace Elements analysis detects small amounts of metals.

Summary And Trends In Water Quality

Principal water quality assessments of this area include the State of Texas Water Quality Inventory and Regional Water Quality Assessments of Water Quality in the Rio Grande Basin (TNRCC, 1994a; TNRCC, 1996a). In addition, the next regional water quality assessment is scheduled to be initiated in 2001 with data collection and assessment through 2004; this report is required by the CRP and will be completed by the IBWC.

Another periodic water quality assessment of the Rio Grande is the Water Quality Inventory (305b Report), which TNRCC completes as mandated by section 305b of the Federal Clean Water Act. TNRCC uses the water quality data from the TNRCC SWQM Program, USGS water quality data and the CRP as well as the information from the bi-national studies to determine the impairment status of the Rio Grande every 2 years (Table 4). The next report will use data from the 5-year period 1996 - 2000 and the 305b report will be used to generate the 303d list of impaired waters, as mandated by section 303d of the Federal Clean Water Act (Christine Kolbe, TNRCC, pers. comm., 2001).

In recent years, two bi-national water quality studies along the Rio Grande from El Paso to Brownsville were conducted, the first in 1992-1993 and the second in 1995 (TNRCC, 1994b; TNRCC, 1997). These studies focused on the presence of toxics in the Rio Grande and major tributaries. The sampling for a third study (from El Paso to Big Bend National Park) has been completed, with a publication by the end of 2001/early 2002.

Table 4. Impairment status for stream segments in the Amistad NRA.

River Reach Name	TNRCC Segment ID	Impairment Cause	Summary of Impairment
Rio Grande Above Amistad Reservoir	2306	Pathogens, Ambient toxicity in water	In the upper 25 miles of the segment, toxicity in water sometimes exceeds the criteria for aquatic life (moderate impairment, partial support). Bacteria levels exceed criteria for contact recreation downstream of Presidio. (Moderate impairment, non support)
Amistad Reservoir	2305		No Impairment
Rio Grande Below Amistad	2304	Pathogens, ambient toxicity in water	Toxicity in water sometimes exceeds criteria for aquatic life downstream of Del Rio and Eagle Pass. Bacteria levels sometimes exceed criteria for contact recreation downstream of Del Rio, Laredo and Eagle Pass. (Moderate Impairment, non support)
Lower Pecos River	2310	Total dissolved solids, sulfate, chloride	Average concentration of chloride, sulfate and total dissolved solids exceed criteria. (Low Impairment, concern)
Devils River	2309		No Impairment

From Draft 2000 Texas Clean Water Act Section 303d List (TNRCC, 2000).

Several studies have also looked at water quality trends in the Rio Grande, using data from both TNRCC and the USGS NASQAN stations. These studies include both a general analysis of trends as well as USGS fact sheets which focus on specific water quality concerns. Water quality monitoring data for the Amistad area is summarized in Table 6.

Water Quality Criteria and Standards

Water quality standards for each river segment are given in Table 5. Standards are site specific to each river segment, and are determined in part upon historical levels of these water quality parameters. Designated beneficial uses for all of these waters include contact recreation and high aquatic life, except for the Devils River, which has an exceptional aquatic life use specified (30 TAC, 307.10). The results of the 2000 assessment of water quality impairment is given in Table 4. Currently, TNRCC is conducting studies of toxicity as part of a statewide toxicity Total Maximum Daily Load project and fish consumption for the Rio Grande Above Amistad as these two standards could not be assessed due to a lack of information.

Table 5. Water Quality Standards for Waters in the Amistad NRA

River Reach Name	Segment Number	Temp. (F/C)	pH Range	Dissolved Oxygen (minimum) (mg/L)	TDS (mg/L)	Chloride (mg/L)	Sulfate (mg/L)
Rio Grande Above Amistad Reservoir	2306	93/34	6.5-9.0	5.0	1550	300	570
Amistad Reservoir	2305	88/31	6.5-9.0	5.0	800	150	270
Rio Grande Below Amistad	2304	95/35	6.5-9.0	5.0	1000	200	300
Lower Pecos River	2310	92/33	6.5-9.0	5.0	4000	1700	1000
Devils River	2309	90/32	6.5-9.0	6.0	300	500	500

Taken from Texas Administrative Code, 30 TAC, 307.10 (1); August 2000

Table 6. Average and Range of Selected Water Quality Parameters for Water Quality Monitoring Stations in the Amistad Area

Water Quality Monitoring Station	Data Source/ Period of Record	Temp (C)	pH	Dissolved Oxygen (mg/L)	Conductivity (uS/cm)	Ammonia (mg/L)	Nitrate + Nitrite (mg/L)	Total Phosphorus (mg/L)	Chloride (mg/L)	Sulfate (mg/L)
Rio Grande at Foster Ranch	USGS NASQAN 96-99	23.3 (9.5-29.0)	8.0 (7.4-8.5)	7.8 (2.6-12.1)	1100 (506-1880)	nd[16] (nd-0.208)	0.716 (nd-1.651)	0.104 (nd-13.55)	109 (27-300)	289 (120-394)
Pecos River at Langtry	USGS NASQAN 96-99	25.0 (10.0-37.0)	8.1 (7.5-8.7)	8.3 (6.3-10.9)	3470 (716-5200)	0.031 (nd-0.270)	0.110 (nd-1.912)	nd (nd-0.070)	752 (102-1300)	472 (68-740)
International Amistad Reservoir Rio Grande Arm	CRP 97-99	20.4 (12.9-28.3)	7.9 (7.7-8.2)	8.8 (7.8-10.5)	1149 (1013-1322)	0.025 (0.025-0.025)	0.373 (0.270-0.520)	0.02 (0.01-0.04)	142 (121-162)	206 (180-257)
International Amistad Reservoir Devils River Arm	CRP 97-99	17.1 (1 sample only)	8.1 (1 sample only)	8.2 (1 sample only)	699 (1 sample only)	0.025 (0.025-0.025)	0.742 (1.01-0.42)	0.02 (0.01-0.04)	50 (32-63)	66 (86-37)
International Amistad Reservoir At Buoy #1, near Dam	CRP 97-98	21.3 (11.3-31.0)	8.1 (7.3-9.4)	7.7 (5.8-10.7)	1127 (972-1221)	0.03 (0.2-0.6)	NA	2.2 (0.1-4.4)	167 (132-206)	222 (181-283)
Devils River at Pafford Crossing nr Comstock	CRP 93-99	19.27 (8.78-27.6)	8.18 (8.1-8.4)	9.76 (8.0-11.8)	389 (367-433)	0.04 (0.01-0.05)	1.07 (0.01-1.44)	0.02 (0.01-0.03)	14.53 (7.0-17.0)	8.41 (1.0-9.36)
Rio Grande below Amistad	USGS NASQAN/ 97-99	19.0 (11.5-26.0)	7.8 (7.2-8.3)	5.8 (1.6-10.01)	1160 (645-1370)	0.020 (nd-0.119)	0.375 (0.109-1.012)	nd (nd-0.080)	157.2 (60.86-200.0)	220.0 (93.66-260.0)

Data from USGS NASQAN Summary Statistics for the Rio Grande Basin (water.usgs.gov/nasqan) and from Texas Clean Rivers Program Data (CRP) (IBWC, 2001).

[16] nd- not detected - below detection limit

Rio Grande Above Amistad (Segment 2306)

As mentioned above, water in this section of the Rio Grande originates both from the Upper Rio Grande (Segments 2307 and 2306) and the Rio Conchos. The river flows through deep canyons and the sparsely populated area along the border with Mexico. Water quality in this part of the Rio Grande reflects the quality of the water from these two rivers. However, historical mine tailings (primarily mercury, silver and lead) are located in the headwaters of several of the tributaries into the Rio Grande above Amistad. When these tributaries flow in response to a rainstorm, heavy metals and other toxins could be washed into the river.

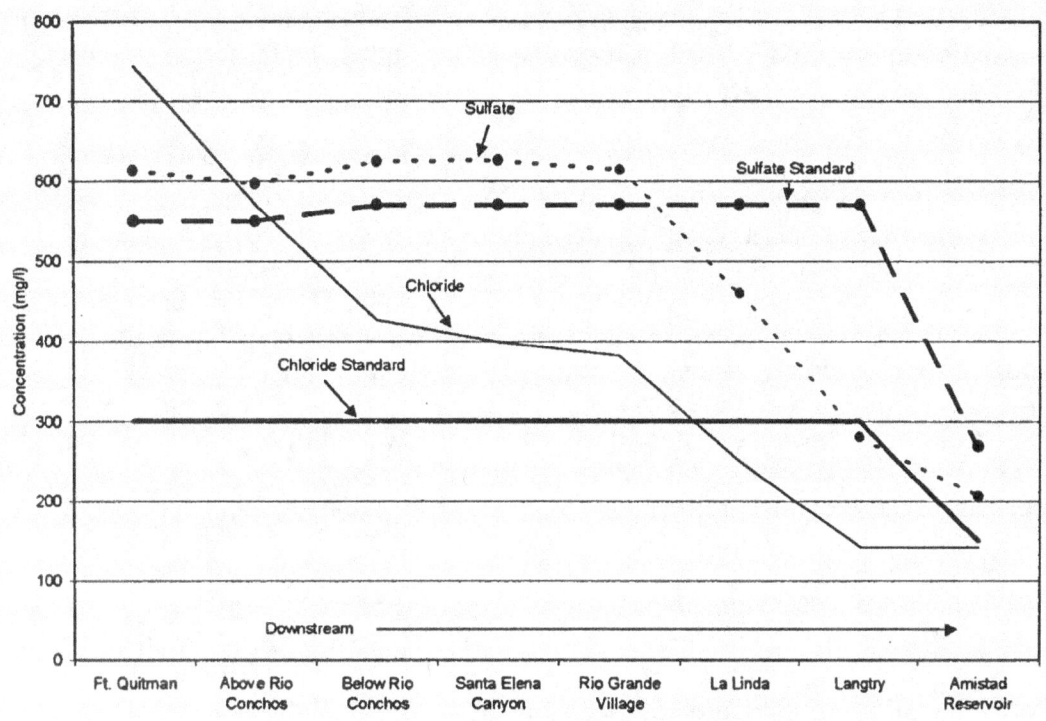

Figure 17. Average Sulfate and Chloride Concentrations (1995-2000) for the Rio Grande Above Amistad. (IBWC, 2001)

Various assessments in the past have identified concerns over elevated concentrations of nutrients, trace elements, and various pesticides in this segment of the river (TNRCC, 1994; 1996). Comparison of NASQAN water quality data for the Rio Grande below the Rio Conchos to the data taken at the Rio Grande at Foster Ranch indicates that concentrations of all of these parameters tends to be much less in the downstream portion of this river segment (USGS, 2001). This is as expected due to the absence of irrigation return flows, industry or municipal discharges to the river between Big Bend National Park and Amistad.

In the upper reaches of this segment, downstream of Presidio and through Big Bend National Park, chloride and sulfate levels often exceed state water quality standards (Figure 17) (IBWC, 2001), which are the cause of occasional toxicity in this part of the river. Downstream of Big Bend National Park, many springs flow into the river in the lower canyons portion of the Rio Grande Wild and Scenic River. The freshwater inflow from these springs are the reason the concentration of chloride and sulfate decrease markedly between La Linda and Langtry, Texas.

Trends
An analysis of riverbed sediment data showed no trends for most trace elements in the Rio Grande between Presidio and Amistad Reservoir (Lee and Wilson, 1997). Mercury and zinc did show an increasing trend since the 1970's.

Over the past 30 years, salinity has been rising in this section of the Rio Grande (Miyamoto, 1995). This is due to the increase in water use upstream, resulting in more concentrated salts from irrigation return flows and municipal wastewater outfalls. Also a greater percentage of the flow into this section of the Rio Grande is coming from the Rio Grande above the Rio Conchos, which has higher salinity than the Rio Conchos. More discussion on both salinity and trace elements can be found below in the Water Resource Issues section.

Pecos River (Segment 2310)
The Pecos River has highly saline water, partially due to a series of saline seeps and springs that flow into the Pecos River in the Malaga Bend area. Reduced freshwater inflows from both over pumping of the groundwater adjacent to the river, and from upstream water regulation have further increased the salinity of the river. State water quality standards for chloride and sulfate are much higher than any other segment in the Rio Grande Basin (Table 5), and the average concentrations of these salts exceed the levels needed to safeguard general water quality uses (TNRCC, 2000).

Disposal of saline water produced from oil wells may also be increasing the salt load in the river. Salt concentrations tend to decrease downstream along the Pecos River due to freshwater inputs to the river. Just upstream of Amistad Reservoir, chloride averaged 752 mg/L and sulfate averaged 473 mg/L in the Pecos River between 1996 and 1999. Conductivity averaged over 3400 us/cm during this period (USGS, 2000). Concentrations decrease in response to rainstorms, and increase during periods of prolonged low flow until the high streamflow event (Figure 18) (IBWC, 2001).

The lower Pecos River supports the beneficial uses of high aquatic life, contact recreation and public water supply. Not enough data were available for TNRCC to assess whether fish consumption criteria were met (TNRCC, 2000).

Sampling at the USGS Nasqan station, Pecos River near Langtry (just upstream of Amistad Reservoir), detected naturally occurring minerals barium, boron, strontium and lithium. Pesticides detected include atrazine, diazinon, terbuthylazin and HCH alpha-D6 (USGS, 1999a).

The 1992 and 1994 water quality assessments by TNRCC identified additional parameters of concern: mercury, silver selenium, and 2,4,5-T. Of these compounds, only mercury appears in the analysis of sediment and fish tissue (TNRCC, 1994a); (Texas Water Commission, 1992).

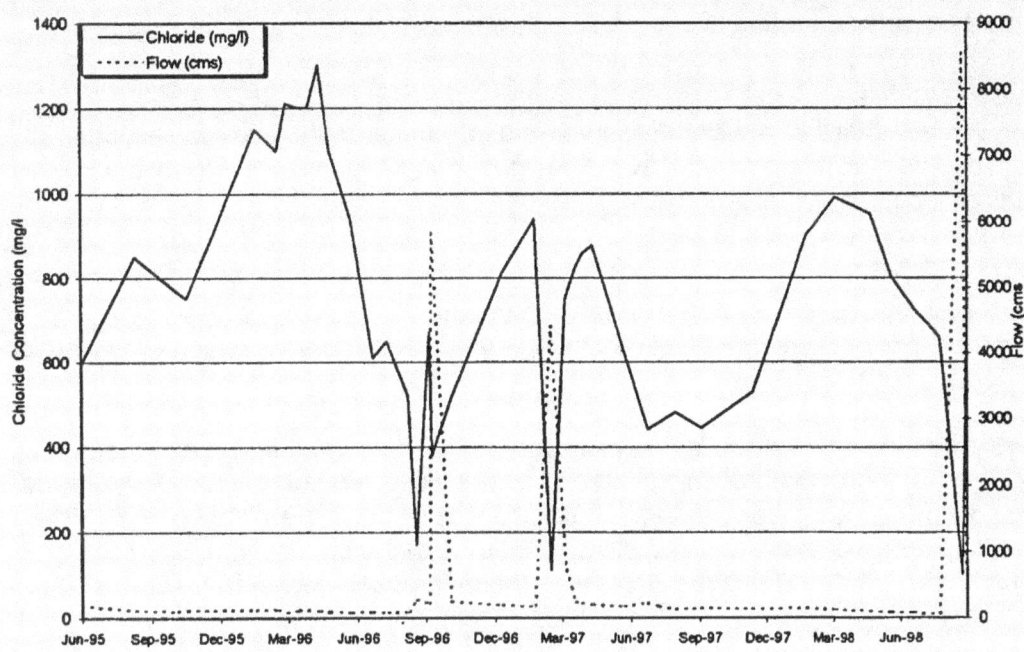

Figure 18. Chloride Concentrations and Streamflow in the Pecos River at Langtry. (from IBWC, 2001)

Large fish kills have been reported on the Pecos, both after large storm events (Jensen, 1987) and during cold weather. Two fish kills in the mid-1980's resulted in over 1/2 million fish killed, primarily sunfish and minnows. A dinoflagellate (Gymnodinium) and a "golden" algae (Pyrmnesium parvum) were detected in water samples taken shortly after the kills. These organisms favor cold temperatures and salty water (Jensen, 1987). More detailed discussion of algae blooms can be found below in the Water Resources Issues section.

Trends
The annual mean salinity of the Pecos River appears to be increasing (Miyamoto et al, 1995). This correlates with the declining flows in the Pecos River. Mercury also appears to be increasing in this river (Lee and Wilson, 1997).

Devils River

The Devils River is a spring fed river in the Edwards Trinity Watershed with no reservoirs or major impoundments within the watershed. What little development exists in the watershed is almost entirely agricultural. No water quality concerns are currently identified (TNRCC, 2000). The river supports the beneficial uses of public water supply, contact recreation, and exceptional aquatic Life. Nitrate and nitrite concentrations tend to be high as the springs which flow into the river are naturally high in these nutrients (TNRCC, 1996a). Salinity is low, in contrast to the other tributaries of the reservoir. Fish consumption risk has not been assessed due to insufficient data.

41

<u>Trends</u>
Water quality data are more limited for the Devils River than the other major rivers in the Amistad area. The available water quality data does not indicate any trends or changes in water quality over time for this river.

Mexican Tributaries

The Mexican tributaries to Amistad Reservoir are intermittent - they flow in response to large rain events. No information is available concerning the water quality or the potential contribution of contaminants from these streams.

Amistad Reservoir

The reservoir fully supports beneficial uses of high aquatic life, contact recreation and public water supply. There was not enough data for TNRCC to assess fish consumption risk (TNRCC, 2000).

Water quality sampling over the last several years of low reservoir levels have shown a pattern of higher levels of chloride, sulfates and total dissolved solids in the Rio Grande Arm (station 15892) and near the dam (station 13211) as compared to the Devils River Arm (station 15893) of the reservoir (IBWC, 2001). With the increasing salinity of the Rio Grande and the Amistad Reservoir in general, the differences between the Devils River Arm and the rest of the lake are likely to become more pronounced.

<u>Trends</u>
Two major water quality issues are apparent in the reservoir. Rising salinity, due to the decrease in reservoir inflows and the increasing salinity of both the Rio Grande and the Pecos River (Miyamoto et al, 1995). The other issue is the increase in metal concentrations in Amistad Reservoir, probably due to atmospheric sources (Van Metre et al, 1997). Both of these issues are addressed in more detail below in the section on Water Resource Issues section.

The pollutants DDT, DDE and DDD were detected at low concentrations in the reservoir, with decreasing levels since the early 1970's, which follows the trend nationwide after the ban on DDT (Lee and Wilson, 1997).

Rio Grande below Amistad Reservoir

Water quality deteriorates as it goes downstream from Amistad reservoir due to industrial and municipal outflows. Below the Cities of Del Rio, Laredo and Eagle Pass, contact recreation use is not supported due to elevated levels of fecal coliform bacteria (TNRCC, 2000). TNRCC assessments in the past have identified concern over chloride, sulfate and TDS; possible concerns for nitrogen, phosphorus, and zinc were also identified (TNRCC, 1994a).

<u>Trends</u>
Water quality just below Amistad Reservoir tends to be high in chloride and nutrients. Several studies have identified an increasing trend in chloride and sulfate in this part of the Rio Grande (Schertz, et al, 1994) probably due to the increasing salinity in Amistad Reservoir. No trends in trace elements were detected in the analysis of riverbed sediments (Lee and Wilson, 1997).

Fisheries/Aquatic Biological Resources

Fisheries are an important resource within Amistad Reservoir. Recreational (i.e. sport) fishing is extremely popular within the United States portion of the reservoir, with both commercial fishing and a limited but growing sport fishery occurring within the Mexican portion of the reservoir. While the NPS is responsible for the recreational facilities, interpretive programs, and the protection of cultural, natural, and historical resources within the United States portion of the reservoir, the fisheries resources are managed under an agreement with the Texas Parks and Wildlife Department (TPWD). TPWD conducts monitoring surveys, promulgates regulations pertaining to fish harvest, conducts fish stocking activities, and works to enhance fisheries habitat within Amistad Reservoir (Jimmy Dean, TPWD, pers. comm., 2000). Recreational use, natural resource protection, commercial fishing and sport fishing activities within the Mexican portion of the reservoir are managed by the Secretariat of Agriculture, Livestock, Rural Development, Fisheries, and Nutrition (SAGARPA). SAGARPA monitors fisheries harvest, enforces fisheries regulations, conducts scientific studies, and manages a fish stocking program targeted at both the commercial and recreational fisheries (Agostin Ramos Arizpe, SEMARNAT, pers. comm., 2000).

For the United States portion of the reservoir, the primary objectives of TPWD are to make sport fishing the best possible while protecting and enhancing the aquatic resources (Jimmy Dean, TPWD, pers. comm., 2000). Currently, more than 100 bass tournaments per year take place within the United States portion of Amistad Reservoir (Bill Sontag, Amistad N.R.A., pers. comm., 2000).

As part of TPWD management activities, fisheries harvest regulations are promulgated to:

- Protect fish from over harvest.
- Protect fish with reproductive or recruitment problems.
- Improve quality of fish harvested by anglers.
- Improve the fish population structure.

Current TPWD harvest regulations for Amistad Reservoir (bag and size limits) pertain to recreational fish species including largemouth bass (*Micropterus salmoides*), striped bass (*Morone saxatilis*), white bass (*Morone chrysops*), smallmouth bass (*Micropterus dolomieui*), blue catfish (*Ictalurus furcatus*), channel catfish (*Ictalurus punctatus*), flathead catfish (*Pylodictus olivaris*), white crappie (*Pomoxis annularis*) and walleye (*Stizostedion vitreum vitreum*) (Zerr, 2000).

The TPWD further conducts fisheries surveys as part of its statewide fisheries monitoring and management program. These surveys are conducted every 3-4 years utilizing a variety of collection techniques including gill nets, trap nets, and electrofishing (Zerr, 2000). Target species within Amistad Reservoir for these surveys include:

- Gill Netting: channel catfish (*Ictalurus punctatus*), flathead catfish (*Pylodictus olivaris*), white bass (*Morone chrysops*), striped bass (*Morone saxatilis*)

- Electrofishing: largemouth bass (*Micropterus salmoides*), gizzard shad (*Dorosoma cepedianum*), redbreast sunfish (*Lepomis auritus*), bluegill (*Lepomis macrochirus*)

- Trap Nets: white crappie *(Pomoxis annularis)*

Information from these fisheries surveys is used both to monitor the quality of the sport fish population and to establish recommended stocking levels for the United States portion of the reservoir. Currently TPWD stocks only striped bass from the Dundee Hatchery (Electra, TX) and Florida largemouth bass from the A.E. Wood Hatchery (San Marcos, TX) into Amistad Reservoir (Jimmy Dean, TPWD, pers. comm., 2000). Table 7 summarizes the historical fish stocking activities of the TPWD into the United States portion of Amistad Reservoir.

Mexico considers Amistad Reservoir as the most important surface water resource within the State of Coahuila. While 90% of the commercial fishing activity in Mexico is marine, the freshwater fishery is an important resource in inland states such as Coahuila. Though primary agricultural activities in this semi-arid state revolve around cattle ranching and farming, the fishery resource can and does provide an important complementary food resource, as well as a locally important source of employment. Two local commercial fishing cooperatives support between 30 and 40 commercial fishermen and a potential exists to boost tourism revenue through a small, but developing sport fishery which currently supports about 2300 annual fishing licenses and 6 – 7 bass tournaments annually.

Currently, the commercial fishery in Amistad Reservoir provides approximately 65% of the fish harvested in the State of Coahuila, with the primary fish species harvested including catfish *(Ictalurus spp.)*, besugo (freshwater drum) *(Aplodinotus grunniens)* , common carp *(Cyprinus carpio)*, cuchilla (gizzard shad) *(Dorosoma cepedianum)*, matalote (smallmouth buffalo)*(Ictiobus bubalus)* and tilapia *(Tilapia aurea)* (Daniel Hernandez Montano, Instituto Nacional de la Pesca (INP), pers. comm. 2000).

SAGARPA regulates the commercial fisheries within the Mexican portion of Amistad Reservoir via a permit system, restricting the number of commercial fishermen, allocating the number of gill nets per fisherman, establishing size limits on fish, and regulating fishing hours. In order to maintain a viable and sustainable commercial fishing industry the number of commercial fishing permits are limited to between 30 and 40 fishermen, all of whom are members of one of two cooperatives, and each fisherman is allowed to have between 3 and 8 gill nets. Nets must be checked every 24 hours and commercial fishing is not allowed on weekends in order that the nets do not interfere with sport fishing activities (Marco A. Ramos Frayjo, SEMARNAT, pers. comm., 2000).

SAGARPA also has a robust fish harvest monitoring program where fisherman must report their catch on a monthly basis complemented by monthly visits from fisheries biologists from the Instituto Nacional de la Pesca (INP) who weigh and measure the harvest and inspect for parasites or other abnormalities in the caught fish. SEGARPA also supports a fish stocking program in the Mexican portion of the reservoir stocking bagre (catfish) *(Ictalurus spp.)*, common carp *(Cyprinus carpio)*, tilapia *(Tilapia aurea)* and largemouth bass *(Micropterus salmoides)* from a fish hatchery located at La Rosa, Coahuila (Arnoldo Martinez Cano, SEGARPA, pers. comm., 2000).

44

Table 7. Historical Fish Stocking Records of the Texas Parks and Wildlife Department for the United States Portion of Amistad Reservoir.

SPECIES	YEARS	TOTAL NUMBER STOCKED
Largemouth bass (*Micropterus salmoides*)	1967 – 1973	3,240,685
Florida largemouth bass (*Micropterus salmoides*)	1975 – present	3,383,706
Smallmouth bass (*Micropterus dolomieui*)	1975 – 1983	665, 250
Striped bass (*Morone saxatilis*)	1974 – present	5,756,733
Hybrid Striped bass (x White bass)	1975 – 1982	344,962
Walleye (*Stizostedion vitreum vitreum*)	1975 – 1978	17,393,000
Channel catfish (*Ictalurus punctatus*)	1967 – 1973	486,020
Blue catfish (*Ictalurus furcatus*)	1971	5,445
White crappie (*Pomoxis annularis*)	1989	144,591
Northern Pike (*Esox lucius*)	1976	1,030,305
Muskellunge (*Esox masquinongy*)	1976	700

(Information from Jimmy Dean, TPWD, pers. comm., 2000)

Table 8. 1998 Commercial Fish Harvest Records of SEMARNAP for the Mexican Portion of Amistad Reservoir

Common Name	Genus species	1998 Commercial Harvest (Metric tonnes)
Bagre (ie channel catfish, white catfish, blue catfish and black bullhead)	*Ictalurus punctatus* *Ictalurus furcatus* *Ictalurus catus* *Ictalurus melas*	69.28
Besugo (i.e. freshwater drum)	*Aplodinutus grunniens*	40.20
Carpa (i.e. common carp)	*Cyprinus carpio*	24.66
Cuchilla (i.e. gizzard shad)	*Dorosoma cepedianum*	8.30
Metalote (i.e. smallmouth buffalo)	*Ictiobus bubalus*	5.03
Tilapia (i.e. blue tilapia)	*Tilapia aurea*	0.50

(Information from Daniel Hernandez Montano, Instituto Nacional de la Pesca (INP), pers. comm. 2000)

WATER-RELATED RESOURCE ISSUES

The following issues were developed through scoping meetings with the staff of Amistad NRA and with the Water Resources Division of the Texas District of the USGS (located in Austin, TX). Literature review and discussions with TNRCC and the IBWC also aided in the evaluation of these issues.

Salinity

Salinity in the Rio Grande above and below Amistad and in the Pecos River has been increasing since at least 1975 (Schertz, 1990). During the growing season, (March 15 to September 15) salinity levels can triple due to irrigation return flows. With increasing salinity of it's tributaries, Amistad Reservoir has had rising salinity since 1983 (Miyamoto et al, 1995)

The Rio Grande is the largest tributary of the reservoir, with the majority of the water coming from the Rio Conchos, which joins the Rio Grande at Presidio, TX. However the Pecos River, and flow from the Rio Grande above the Rio Conchos contribute significantly more to the salt-loading of the reservoir due to the high salinity of both of these rivers as compared to the Rio Conchos (Table 9).

Salinity levels in the Rio Grande above the Rio Conchos vary with the amount of rainfall. During wet years, rainfall dilutes the concentration of salts in the river from irrigation return flows and municipal wastewater discharges from El Paso and Ciudad Juarez. Salinity levels in the other river reaches follow this same pattern with the exception of large flow events. High salinity has been measured during and after high flow events on the Rio Conchos and the Pecos River. Periods of high flows saturate stream banks, leaching salts into the river as the flow recedes (Miyamoto et al, 1999). Salinity is higher during low flows just after a high flow event, indicating that the salts are leached from streambanks into the river during floods, and then are carried downstream during and after the high flow event.

Table 9. Salt loading of Amistad Reservoir between 1969 to 1989.

River Section	Water Quality Station	Mean Annual Flow (acre-feet / million cubic meters)	Salt Concentration (mg/L)
Rio Grande Above Rio Conchos	Ft Quitman	136,890 / 169	2083
Rio Conchos	Near Ojinaga	736,290 / 909	839
Pecos River	Langtry	221,940 / 274	1985
Devils River	Pafford Crossing	285,930 / 353	264
Rio Grande Below Amistad	Below Amistad Dam	1,671,030 / 2063	656

(adapted from Miyamota et al, 1995)

Salinity levels in Amistad Reservoir are reduced somewhat by the inflow of fresh water from the Devils River and freshwater springs under and adjacent to the reservoir. However, salinity levels in the reservoir are rising at a rate of 15 mg/L per year (Miyamoto et al, 1995). Calculations of salt inflow and outflow of Amistad Reservoir indicate that there may be a continuing accumulation of salts in the reservoir. This is due to the continuing drought (since 1993) where the Pecos River is providing a greater proportion of reservoir inflows than historically. Also, flows from the comparatively fresh water Rio Conchos have been diminished. Historically, the Rio Conchos provided 80% of the flow in the Rio Grande, but since 1993 has only contributed about 50%. Thus much less fresh water is flowing into the system to dilute the salts contributed by the Rio Grande above the Rio Conchos and the Pecos River. In a few years salinity at Amistad Reservoir may have a significant impact on irrigated crops and drinking water downstream (Miyamoto et al, 1995). Salinity levels in the Rio Grande and Pecos are currently high (IBWC, 2001), indicating that salinity levels in the reservoir are probably still increasing.

Nutrients

High levels of nitrogen and phosphorus can cause excessive growth of algae and other aquatic plants. This can result in an imbalance between dissolved oxygen production and consumption. Excessive growth of plankton and algae blooms cause the production of extremely high levels of dissolved oxygen during daytime due to photosynthesis. When photosynthesis ceases during nighttime, these same organisms and other aquatic life consume oxygen, causing oxygen levels to drop. During periods of low flow and warm temperatures, oxygen levels can drop to critically low levels in nutrient rich systems. Fish kills can result as well as impacts on other aquatic life.

High nutrient levels can also alter the species composition and diversity of aquatic life. These nutrients are present in fertilizers and human and animal waste. They can enter the river from irrigation return flows, feedlot runoff and treated municipal wastewater.

Phosphorus is listed as a concern or potential concern for the Rio Grande above Amistad and for Amistad Reservoir. Sources could include irrigation return flows and municipal wastewater, originating primarily in the Rio Conchos and the Rio Grande above Presidio. Nitrates are listed as a concern for the Devils River, although the source is springs that flow naturally into the Devils River (TNRCC, 1994a).

Dissolved oxygen levels have been high enough to support aquatic life however nutrient levels would be expected to increase with the increasing use of water for municipal and agricultural use upstream of Amistad.

Metals and Trace Elements

The two binational toxic studies, the USGS NASQAN stations and several studies, which analyzed sediment, have detected a variety of metals and trace elements in Amistad Reservoir and it's tributaries. Table 10 lists all the substances detected.

Two studies have looked at trends in metals in sediments. A USGS study analyzed trends using data collected by TNRCC sampling and other assessments between 1970 and 1994 (Lee and Wilson, 1997).. This analysis indicates that most trace elements levels appear to be steady, although mercury concentrations are increasing in both the Pecos River, the Rio Grande above Amistad and in Amistad Reservoir. Selenium is also increasing in Amistad Reservoir. The only trace elements with a decreasing trend are copper in Amistad Reservoir and silver in the Pecos River (Lee and Wilson, 1997).

In another study, sediment cores were sampled from both the Rio Grande Arm and the Devils River Arm (Van Metre, et al, 1997). Eight metals (arsenic, chromium, copper, lead, mercury, nickel, vanadium and zinc) have statistically significant increasing trends in the

47

Rio Grande Arm. Both mercury and nickel more than doubled between 1969 and 1995. All but lead and chromium were found to be increasing in the Devils River Arm of the reservoir. All of these metals are associated with atmospheric sources such as burning of fossil fuels and incineration of solid waste (Van Metre, et al, 1997). Elevated levels of arsenic have been detected in water samples and mercury in fish (TNRCC, 1997). Arsenic occurs naturally in the Rio Grande Basin and is especially high in West Texas due to the mineralization of volcanic rock.

Table 10. Metals detected in water, sediment and fish tissue. Values detected above the TNRCC screening level are in bold. (no information is available for the Devils River).

Metals	Rio Grande above Amistad	Pecos River	Amistad Reservoir	Rio Grande below Amistad
Aluminum	water, **sediment**, fish		water, sediment, fish	
Antimony	**water**, fish		**water, sediment**	
Arsenic	**water, sediment**	sediment	**water, sediment, fish**	sediment
Beryllium	water, **sediment**		water, **sediment**	
Cadmium	water, **sediment, fish**		**water, sediment,** fish	fish
Chromium	water, sediment, fish		water, **sediment,** fish	fish
Copper	water, **sediment, fish**		water, **sediment,** fish	**fish**
Lead	water, **sediment, fish**	sediment	water, sediment	sediment, fish
Mercury	water, **sediment,** fish	sediment	water, **sediment, fish**	sediment, fish
Nickel	water, **sediment**		water, **sediment,** fish	
Selenium	**water, sediment, fish**	sediment	water, sediment, fish	sediment, fish
Silver	water,		water, **sediment**	
Thallium	**water**		water, **sediment,** fish	
Zinc	**water, sediment, fish**		water, **sediment,** fish	fish

From Phase II Binational Study, (1997) and from Lee and Wilson (1997).

Algae and Algae blooms

Algae are primarily single celled organisms found ubiquitously throughout the world, but are most abundant in aquatic systems. Most freshwater algae belong to the group Chlorophyta or green algae. Most of the single-celled algae are free floating phytoplankton, while many are filamentous multicellular forms, which attach to rocks and other solid surfaces. Some algae have broad and flexible requirements for their habitat, including temperature, salinity, light, oxygen and carbon dioxide, nutrients, and water movement. Amistad provides an amazing diversity of physical, chemical, and connected biological systems that provides opportunity for many of the broad requirement algae while also nurturing very select and narrow condition locations that likely favor more select algal communities.

In freshwater and marine environments, only a few dozen algal species are considered harmful, because of toxins present during their growth or released upon their death. The best known problem algae are some of the dinoflagellates, which include those responsible for red tides and the toxic *Pfiesteria* species. Some less common groups include some of the diatoms and several of the blue-green algae. Many federal studies of algae bloom problems have focussed on marine and estuary areas because of shellfish concerns, but there is recognition of health and economic factors in freshwater, particularly drinking water in the United States interior. (National Science and Technology Center, 2000)

Algae blooms appear to be an issue primarily in the Pecos River. Algae blooms have not been documented in the reservoir to date, although algal blooms have occurred in the Rio Grande through the Lower Canyons above the reservoir. Large algal blooms associated with fish kills have occurred several times on the Pecos, usually during cold weather. A dinoflagellate (*Gymnodinium*) and a "golden" alga (*Pyrmnesium parvum*) were detected in water samples taken shortly after the kills (Jensen, 1987).

Gymnodinium is related to the organism that causes toxic red tides in the ocean. Golden algae have some identifiable habitat characteristics. They usually favor brackish or salty water with dissolved solids concentrations in the 13,000 mg/L range but are most toxic in less salty waters. Unlike most algae, they favor cold weather and often appear after the first frost of the year when many warm-weather algae have died. Higher concentrations of calcium, sodium, and magnesium make these algae more toxic. The golden algae produce toxic chemicals that enter the bloodstream of the fish, hemorrhage the gill filaments, and cause them to burst. This blocks oxygen transfer and the fish suffocate (Jensen, 1987).

While no studies of the algae of Amistad reservoir and most of its land area and springs have been completed, algae have been implicated in several fish kills in the Pecos and Rio Grande adjacent to the reservoir. Fish kills are probably the most common reason that algae are investigated in aquatic systems. Fish are sensitive to dissolved oxygen deficits in rivers and lakes, when an overabundance of algae critically depresses oxygen levels in the water, due to nighttime respiration and frequently in combination with higher water temperatures. Certain algae also release specific toxins in aquatic systems during seasonal periods, in response to nutrient conditions, or upon death of large masses of the algae which affects fish survival.

In Amistad Reservoir, as in all aquatic environments, algae tend to grow faster and more abundantly when temperatures rise and nutrients abound. Thus, a warm reservoir, such as Amistad, receiving any increasing loads of nutrients from local or river delivered land runoff, wastewater treatment discharges, or leaking septic systems might experience increases in algal growth or blooms of nuisance species. These algae can provide a food source for zooplankton and eventually fish, but also can be a source of toxins or cause of oxygen starvation for fish in portions of the reservoir.

Organic Compounds

In the Amistad area, the most common dissolved pesticides found in rivers are atrazine and diazinon (commonly used insecticides used both in homes and for agriculture), although a variety of compounds have been detected (Table 11). A USGS study which analyzed sediment core data from Amistad and other Rio Grande Reservoirs found that concentrations of DDT and it's derivatives DDE and DDD in sediment decreased since the 1970's in Amistad Reservoir. No other temporal trend data are available. A study using semi-permeable membrane devices found that pesticide occurrence and concentration in water appear to increase in a downstream direction on the Rio Grande (Moring, 1999). The primary sources of organic compounds for the Amistad area are irrigation return flows and municipal wastewater outflows from the Rio Grande and Rio Conchos above Presidio, Texas and from the upper Pecos River.

Table 11. Percent of Samples Where Dissolved Pesticides Were Detected in Water at USGS NASQAN Stations in the Amistad Area.

Pesticide Detected	Rio Grande at Foster Ranch 96-99	Pecos River near Langtry 96-99	Rio Grande below Amistad Reservoir 97-99
Atrazine	22	16	41
Cyanazine	4		
Dacthal (DCPA)	10	4	3
p, p, DDE	8		
Desethyl atrazine	2		
Diazinon	27	4	10
Metolachlor	4		
Parathion	2		
Prometon	6		10
Pronamide	4		
Propachlor		2	
Simazine	4	4	7
Terbacil		4	
Trifluralin		4	

Information from Summary Statistics for Nasqan Stations (USGS, 2000).

Bacteria

TNRCC quarterly monitoring of the reservoir has detected bacterial levels well within state water quality standards. Flood waters, especially from the Rio Grande bring in high levels of bacteria. Bacterial levels decrease as the flood waters travel into the reservoir due to dilution of the flood waters, however high levels may persist for several days in the Rio Grande arm of the reservoir.

A more probable source of bacterial contamination originating from the reservoir is from the dump stations at the marina facilities. This is discussed in more detail under the marina operations section.

Water Quality during Flood Events

Flood events can carry a variety of pollutants into the reservoir. As discussed above, floods can leach salts from streambanks and contribute significantly to the salt loading of the reservoir. Flood waters are typically high in nutrients and bacteria, and are highly turbid.

Toxins can be washed into the river by flood events. Historical mining has occurred in most of the tributaries of the Rio Grande above Amistad. Athough not confirmed, contaminated mine tailings may be washed into the Rio Grande during large rainstorms. Other sources of pollution include municipal sewage systems, which have a history of being overwhelmed by rainstorms, contributing raw sewage into the river. Fish kills on the Rio Grande and the Pecos have occurred during these high flow events, often after a period of prolonged low flow; the cause of the fish mortality is unknown at this time.

An assessment of the USGS NASQAN data for the past several years indicates some correlation in water quality during high flows:

In the Pecos River, two high flow events were sampled between 1996 and 1998. Water quality data from both events show an increase in the concentration of nutrients, and decreases in the concentration of major ions and trace elements (USGS, 1999a). It appears that pesticides are more likely to be detected during a high flow than during a low flow, possibly indicating that rainstorms may wash some contaminants into the Pecos River that do not normally reach the river during dry periods.

The Rio Grande at Foster Ranch has had several high flow events between 1996 and 1998. During flood events of about 1,000 cfs (28.3 cms), nutrients and conductivity increase, as do some of the major ions (USGS, 1999b). In large peakflow events, these parameters decrease, probably due to the increase in water from the Rio Conchos, which tends to have lower concentrations of these constituents than does the Rio Grande. The concentration of trace elements and the percent detection of pesticides do not appear to be correlated with floods (USGS, 1999b).

Fluctuating Reservoir Water Levels

Effects on Threatened and Endangered species

Least Terns
The interior least tern (*Sterna antillarum*), listed as an endangered species in 1985 (USFWS, 1995), has been documented as a breeder at Amistad Reservoir since 1988 (Sorola, 1988). Nesting habitat for the tern occurs on islands that form in the reservoir with fluctuating water levels. Nesting has occurred throughout the reservoir from Buoy 20 in the Rio Grande Arm to sites near Buoy G in the Devils River Arm. Islands that appear from lowering water levels during the spring water release seem to be the preferred sites for breeding. Terns primarily nest on islands with gravel substrate and no vegetation or fire ants. Water withdrawal from the reservoir occurs usually in March/April in order to supply agricultural needs downstream. This directly benefits the terns in respect to new islands appearing with no vegetation or ants during their arrival to the reservoir in late April/early May. Problems arise when water levels in the reservoir increase in the summer and flood the nesting islands. This occurs when water demands downstream are not needed and the release of water is reduced. During the 1999 breeding season, water levels increased to a point that potentially caused the loss of young of the year at three breeding islands.

51

Approximately 120 adult terns have been documented during the breeding season on the United States side of the Amistad Reservoir during the 1999 breeding season. During the 2000 breeding season, a full survey of the Amistad reservoir was conducted on 7/18/00. A total of 273 adults and 71 juveniles were documented (Larson, 2000). On the U.S. side, 88 adults and 21 juveniles were documented. On the Mexico side, 185 adults and 50 juveniles were documented. The recovery plan for the interior least tern states the recovery objective for the tern to be "current number of adult birds in the Rio Grande River system (500) will remain stable for 10 years" (Sidle and Harrison, 1990).

Effects on Aquatic Biological Resources

Currently, a primary concern of both Mexican and United States resource managers are the low lake levels brought about by regional drought conditions over the last 7 years. Amistad Reservoir was last at its conservation level (1117 ft) (340.5) in 1993 and in September, 2000 was approximately 48 (14.6 m) feet below this level. The low lake levels are a concern to fisheries managers because they result in a loss of cover and habitat; may have deleterious effects on reproduction, survival, and recruitment of fish species; and increase susceptibility to gill nets when the lake becomes confined to the former river channel (Jimmy Dean, TPWD, pers. comm., 2000). Similarly, the severely declining water levels have most likely adversely affected freshwater mussel populations and/or those of the fish host of its larval stage (Robert Howells, TPWD, pers. comm., 2000).

Effects on Migratory Fauna

Amistad Reservoir is located along the central migratory flyway for birds moving to and from temperate locations. Many rare bird species are observed passing through Amistad NRA on their migrational movements. White-faced Ibis (*Plegadis chihi*) (Species of Concern), black tern (*Childonias niger*) (Species of Concern), and bald eagles (*Haliaeetus leucocephalus*) (Threatened Species) are observed on occasion moving through the area (USFWS, 1999). Post breeding dispersal of birds also provides the occasional sighting of brown pelican (*Pelecanus occidentalis*) (Endangered Species). All these species are infrequent visitors to the reservoir and are usually only observed for short periods.

Many species of ducks are observed at Amistad NRA during the winter months. The occurrence of hydrilla and other aquatic vegetation in the reservoir attracts many species of ducks which will begin to arrive at the reservoir in late October and early November. Over 20 species can be observed foraging along shorelines on vegetation and invertebrates. By early April most ducks have moved north to temperate locations and many shorebirds are migrating through the area feeding along the shoreline. The permanent presence of a lake system is beneficial to many aquatic bird species by providing an overwintering site and migration corridor where food is easily accessible.

The permanent presence of a fluctuating lake shoreline system is beneficial to many aquatic and shorebird species by providing habitat for overwintering, migration stopovers, and breeding. Two shorebird species that breed during the summer months at the Amistad Reservoir and depend directly on fluctuating water levels for foraging and nesting habitat include the Snowy Plover (*Charadrius alexandrinus*) and the Black-necked Stilt (*Himantopus mexicanus*).

Effects on Archeological Sites

It is estimated that there are more than 1,500 cultural resource sites adjacent to the more than 540 mile (870 kilometer) shoreline on the United States side of Amistad Reservoir.

These resources span more than 10,000 years of Native American prehistory and include historic remains associated with the 19th century Southern Transcontinental Railroad and early 20th century ranching. Prehistoric archeological sites are the most common, with an estimated 900 sites within the immediate flood pool of the reservoir (Labadie, 1994).

Prior to the impoundment of waters behind Amistad Reservoir in 1969, there had been over 10 years of archeological fieldwork, which inventoried and documented sites that would be inundated by the future reservoir. Over 300 major prehistoric sites were documented. Twenty-two sites, mostly caves and dry rockshelters were excavated; several sites had more than 20 feet (6 m) of cultural deposits (Anderson, 1974). The pre-inundation research generated more than 4,000 photographs, 65 linear feet (20 m) of documents, and produced a museum collection estimated to contain more than 1,000,000 artifacts, all of which are now managed by the park.

In the Spring of 1994, lake levels began dropping in response to what would become a multi-year, regional drought affecting most of southwest Texas and northeastern Mexico. By the Summer of 1998, Amistad Reservoir had dropped 56 vertical feet (17 m) and covered less than 20% of the area it did at normal operating levels. Since 1994, Archeological surveys in drawdown zones have documented over 150 new archeological sites and re-documented nearly 50 sites identified by the pre-inundation research.

Many of the recently discovered sites initially appeared as silt-covered mounds of fist-sized rocks rising above the unvegetated mud flats; some were unapproachable because of the quicksand-like nature of the mud. These new sites range from the isolated remains of a single prehistoric campfire pit to sites covering over 5 acres (2 hectares) that have several hundred campfire pits, tipi rings, and grinding holes (Labadie, 1999). The overall shape of these features, circular concentrations of tightly packed fire-cracked rock, are intermixed with darker soils, suggesting that many may still have intact archeological deposits despite nearly 30 years of inundation. Intermixed within these soils are small, modern Asiatic clam shells (*Corbicula fluminea*). Because of its widespread distribution throughout the reservoir, continuous burrowing behavior, and high population densities, the Asiatic clam is adversely affecting most submerged archeological sites throughout the entire reservoir basin (Shafer et al, 1997)

More than 1500 individual fire-cracked rock features have been documented since 1994, nearly all of which have been significantly affected by wave-action from high winds, passing boats, and fluctuations in reservoir levels. It is now believed that the modern ground slope of exposed terraces is a basic determinant of the severity of wave-action damage to all archeological sites or individual features. An optimum ground slope angle appears to exist where wave action effects are negligible; above or below this angle, wave action is intensified resulting in somewhat predictable dispersal patterns across recently exposed ground surfaces (Collins and Labadie, 1999)

Typically, sites with ground slopes above eight degrees will have a series of individual cut-banks often resembling stair-steps with each step representing a different lake elevation. Sites with low ground slope angles usually have a parallel series of drift lines or windrows (similar to high-tide lines at the beach) composed of *corbicula* shells, chert flakes, and small fraction fire-cracked rocks (Labadie, 1999). In either setting, horizontal relationships among artifacts or feature specific lithic associations are highly suspect given the number of times most sites have been subjected to the cycle of inundation, exposure, and re-inundation.

It is also becoming clear that wave-action differentially affects the various classes of archeological materials at recently exposed archeological sites (Gustavson and Collins, 2000). Small items, such as flint flakes and arrowheads, bone or shell fragments and organic materials are the first to be relocated as wave passes across the site. Larger items, such as metates or rock-lined cooking pits, require greater amounts of wave-energy to move individual items or before the waves systematically dissemble a fire-cracked rock feature. It has also been demonstrated that as a wave sweeps across an ancient campfire or cooking pit, it is capable of dislodging the associated soil matrix and, over time, can fill these voids between the rocks entirely with modern lacustrine deposits. The result of this process is that although a fire-cracked rock feature may look intact, the interior deposits can be entirely modern (Collins et al, 2000).

The regional drought that has gripped the Amistad NRA has been making national headlines for several years now. Visitation has dropped substantially and the reservoir has receded to its lowest levels since it began filing in the late 1960s. On the brighter side of things, the drought has provided archeologists and other earth scientists an unprecedented opportunity to study a portion of the prehistoric landscape thought to have been long lost under the waters of Amistad Reservoir.

Water Quality Related to Changes in Reservoir Level

There is little data on the changes in Amistad Reservoir water quality resulting from water level changes. Water quality changes from floods, which often will increase water level are discussed above. Other potential changes would be from high water washing trash into the reservoir and from large mats of hydrilla dying as a result of being submerged too deeply to survive. The decaying organic matter from trash and dead hydrilla may locally increase nutrients and lower dissolved oxygen. Other contaminants would enter the reservoir when trash dumped in arroyos around the reservoir is submerged.

No algae blooms or water color changes have been documented as a result of changes in reservoir level.

Shoreline Erosion Related to Water Level Fluctuations

Rockfalls are common in the limestone cliffs surrounding the reservoir. It is likely that the rock is degrading more rapidly due to the repeated inundations. This could be degrading rock shelters and other archeological remains, as well as accelerating a natural geologic process.

Effects On Reservoir Use And On Amistad Facilities And Operations

Currently, only two boat ramps are fully usable at low water levels, Diablo East and Rough Canyon. A paved boat ramp at Box Canyon was completed during the summer of 2000 to a reservoir water depth of 1,080 feet. Ramp extensions are scheduled for year 2001 to make this ramp a low water level boat launch site. Spur Roads 454 and 277, old roads that were submerged by the reservoir provide boat access at most water levels. However fluctuating reservoir levels have degraded the pavement and resurfacing is not an option as the asphalt would leach toxins into the reservoir when the road is submerged at higher water levels.

The Pecos boat ramp has not been usable in recent years except by small boats due to low lake levels. The recreational use at this facility has dropped significantly due to the lack of access caused by increased sedimentation in this area. A temporary wooden boat ramp was constructed during the Spring of 2001 to allow access for small boats. The vegetation has narrowed the channel to the reservoir from the boat ramp, so the channel would need to be dredged to allow larger boat access.

With the decline in usable boat ramps, there are not enough ramps and parking near launch sites during holiday weekends and other high use periods, resulting in long waits for boaters to launch.

Falling lake levels have left swim beaches and boat access campsites high and dry. Recreational opportunities and use of the NRA has declined as a result. Low water level, in combination with silt deposition is threatening the access to Panther Cave, a major archeological site and visitor attraction at Amistad NRA.

Additionally, rapidly changing lake levels increase the workload of the NRA staff as docks, buoys and other facilities need to be moved to adjust to the new level.

Contamination From Trash Dumped Around The Reservoir

Subdivisions around the lake do not have adequate trash removal for household garbage and other wastes. Refuse is often piled adjacent to subdivision entrances or is illegally dumped into gullies or sinkholes that drain into the reservoir. Some ranches adjacent to the reservoir continue to use the heads of gullies or sinkholes that drain into the reservoir to dump household garbage, dead animals and ranch generated trash.

Effects on Aquatic Plants and Biotic Community

Very little is known concerning the effect of fluctuating reservoir level on aquatic biology of Amistad Reservoir. Rooted aquatic plants would be affected with changing levels as deepening water may reduce their ability to photosynthesize, and receding water levels may dessicate the plants. The aquatic biology of the lake would likely be more affected by the increases in temperature and salinity of the lake that occur when lake level decrease.

Exotic Species

Hydrilla

Hydrilla (*Hydrilla verticillata*), also known by the common name Florida elodea is found widely in Amistad Reservoir. It is common throughout the reservoir but predominantly found in large floating mats in sheltered embayments (Figure 19).

Hydrilla was first observed in the reservoir in the 1980's probably arriving through one of the contributing rivers or through recreational boating from other water bodies. It has since become a notable nuisance to boaters.

Hydrilla is an aggressively spreading dicot plant, reproducing from turions (winter buds), tubers, and fragmentation. It is a common aquatic plant used in aquariums and may have entered many water systems through this use. Originally a subtropical Asian native, hydrilla was first observed in 1960 in Florida. It has staked out a strong presence now throughout temperate climates in the southern United States; spreading north and commonly found in Delaware and observed even in Connecticut. It is found throughout Texas, much of Mexico, and along the U.S. Pacific coast in California and Washington.

55

Hydrilla is difficult to control in most aquatic systems in the United States, because of the lack of native controls, and hydrilla's amazing adaptations to reproduce and survive. It can be rooted to the bottom or grow in a mat-like floating mass. Hydrilla variously produces hybernacula, turions in leaf axils, and tubers on rhizomes. It thrives in fresh and brackish waters either flowing or stagnant and throughout a wide pH range. It is also very light tolerant, growing to depths of 50 feet (15 m). It competes very effectively for sunlight, and thrives in both high and low nutrient systems.

Hydrilla growth and mats negatively affects recreational users of the reservoir
Many motorboating activities (fishing and water skiing) are interrupted by when propellers become tangled in the mats of hydrilla. While no apparent permanent harm is caused, the entanglements cause visitor complaints and pose a possible hazard to boat operators removing the weeds from the boat motors or potentially to swimmers getting entangled in the weeds. Despite observable benefits to largemouth bass habitat in years past, there is concern by sport fishermen and researchers that negative affects generally appear when hydrilla coverage exceeds 30% in aquatic systems like Amistad. Hydrilla is known to provide shelter to several of the game fish in the reservoir, but also appear to be partially responsible for the decline of panfish and bass populations.

In riverine systems, including the lower Rio Grande River, hydrilla has caused severe flow restrictions, interfering with normal current and irrigation delivery success, flood capacity, and the sediment carrying ability of the river.

Observed from a boat on Amistad reservoir, hydrilla tends to form in small to large mats (up to 100 feet (32 m) across) that are difficult to see. Under some lighting and wave size conditions the mats are nearly invisible. From the air, the mats are readily discerned as dark green to black areas on the water throughout the main portion of the reservoir and its side inlets. Larger hydrilla mats have been most common when water levels remain stable or dropping for extended periods of time. The conditions under which hydrilla appears to be less of an impact on visitors or boaters has been on rising water levels that keep ahead of hydrilla's growth. Naturally, vegetative growth does eventually catch up with such water level changes; thus the relief is only temporary.

Treatment of hydrilla in aquatic systems has been performed historically throughout the United States with: herbicides (chelated copper compounds, diquat dibromide, and fluridone); grass carp, and; mechanical removal. Various natural control organisms (snails, weevils, leaf mining flies, aquatic moths) have been released to control hydrilla with some success and others are under development (Center, 1992). Managed water level control has shown partial success in some lake systems, when hydrilla is prevented from forming tubers in the fall and vegetative regrowth and sprouting of fibers in the spring (Haller et al, 1976). The U.S. Bureau of Reclamation (BOR) has been investigating the spread and impacts of hydrilla and other exotic aquatic plants (water hyacinth and salt cedar) in sections of the Rio Grande below Amistad Reservoir and at Falcon Reservoir. Reduction of river flow through large mats of floating and rooted exotic plants has disrupted flow delivery for power and irrigation, caused channel sedimentation increases, and caused flooding. During the Summer of 2001, BOR and the U.S. Army Corps of Engineers (COE) will sample Amistad Reservoir and lower sections of the river for these plants and identify potential release points for biological control organisms (pers. Communication, Gordon Mueller USBOR, 2001).

Figure 19. Hydrilla Mats Along the Lakeshore

Figure 20. Exotic Aoudad Sheep on Cliffs above the Reservoir

Salt Cedar

Salt cedar or tamarisk (*Tamarix spp.*) is represented by four species along the Rio Grande (Powell, 1998). Salt cedar is very common in Amistad NRA and is found along the reservoir shoreline and in riparian zones of the Rio Grande and Pecos River. Due to poor soils, salt cedar is uncommon along the upper reaches of the Devils River. Salt cedar is the most common of exotic plants found in the inundation zone of the reservoir. The inundation zone covers approximately 19,000 acres (7,687 hectares) at the 2000 reservoir elevation of 1,081 feet (329 m). It occupies large areas of the inundation zone when water in the reservoir is low. Salt cedar is rare to absent in many areas of the inundation zone where soils are shallow and limestone forms outcrops. This can be found in the Langtry-Rock outcrop association (LRG), the Zorra-Rock outcrop complex (ZoE) with 8 to 15 percent slope, and the Zorra-Rock outcrop complex (ZoD) with a 1 to 8 percent slope. These soil types are very common along many reaches of the shoreline.

Large areas of shoreline where slope is moderate and soils are developed is where large concentrations of salt cedar can be found. Contour levels of salt cedar are found in many areas where the trees germinate as the water levels drops in the reservoir and then stabilizes for weeks to months. These bands of salt cedar provide habitat for many species of birds and also control erosion caused by wave action. Along the upper reaches of the Rio Grande, willow species (*Salix spp.*) have been observed to shade out salt cedar. In these areas, salt cedar is observed along the shoreline of the river, but the floodplain is mainly occupied by willow.

Operational problems with salt cedar have occurred at the Pecos River boat launch. Low water from 1996 to 2000 has allowed salt cedar to overgrow the boat launch area and docks, which are now sitting on sediment deposited by the Rio Grande. Salt cedar has overgrown the silt deposited floodplain of the Pecos River which is currently above the present reservoir water level.

River Cane

River cane, carrizo, and giant reed are all used as common names for (*Arundo donax*). This bamboo like perennial with thick rhizomes is non-native to Texas. Originally introduced from Asia to control erosion along roads, this reed now can be found throughout most of the sand bars and levees of the Rio Grande.

River cane mainly occurs along the upper reaches of the park along the Rio Grande. River cane also occurs below the dam and along the Pecos River. Between the upper reaches of the park boundary on the Rio Grande and the confluence with the Pecos River is where heavy cane growth occurs. Competition with native willow (*Salix spp.*) and salt cedar (*Tamarix spp.*) keeps the cane restricted to large clumps in many areas where the river floodplain is wide. This isn't always the case and river cane can be found as a monoculture occupying the whole floodplain, limiting native plant growth. During floods, river cane is susceptible to water erosion and can become a hindrance to boat traffic. In the 1980's, three large river cane mats formed following flood events. In 1986, a large mat covered the entire width of the Rio Grande at the Pecos river confluence, extended over one-half mile (0.8 km), and prevented boat use. This mat lasted for over four months, effecting the Pecos River and sections of the Rio Grande. Depending on wind, these cane mats will move up and down sections of the river, causing short term closures to boat use. River cane growth along the shoreline of the reservoir is non-existent. Fluctuating water levels prevents the cane from occupying this area.

Asian Clam

Asiatic clams (*Corbicula fluminea*) were first documented in North America in 1924 and have spread throughout nearly all freshwater localities across the United States, limited only by cold water temperatures. The Asiatic clam can be found in high numbers throughout Amistad Reservoir. The clam prefers a well-oxygenated sand and mud bottom habitat in quiet water, usually at depths of 2 to 3.3 feet (0.6 to 1.0 m), but can occur as deep as 39 feet (12m) (Shaffer et.al, 1997). The clams burrow downward into sediments until nearly completely covered and then will move laterally through the matrix as they feed. When the reservoir water level drops, Asiatic clams will burrow deeper to remain submerged. Since Asiatic clams live in dense populations ranging from up to 100 adults to

58

131,000 juveniles per square meter, continued burrowing will displace sediments, and could displace small artifacts and organic materials in submerged archeological sites (Shaffer et al, 1997).

Nutria

Nutria (*Myocastor coypus*) can be found throughout Amistad Reservoir occupying the shoreline zone. Native to South America, nutrias were introduced widely into Texas as a means to control vegetation. The nutrias preference of food in the reservoir is unknown at this time, but their natural food consists mainly of aquatic and semi-aquatic vegetation (Davis and Schmidly, 1994). Nutria have been documented to eat shellfish and have a high preference for sedges, reeds and cattails. Effects of nutria on the resources at Amistad NRA are unknown. The main problem with nutria is their high reproductive capacity, which can soon result in overpopulation and resource damage. Fluctuating water levels may prevent this animal from over-populating the reservoir. Destruction of native vegetation by this animal is not apparent due to the animals existence in the inundation zone. Poor soils and limestone outcrops reduce the presence of many aquatic and semi-aquatic vegetation that nutrias prefer. This may also keep the nutria population from increasing due to poor forage quality.

Wildlife

Amistad NRA has documented very few exotic wildlife species inside the park. A few wild boar have been observed, but the main animals present inside Amistad NRA are the mouflon sheep (*Ovis musimon*) and the aoudad sheep (*Ammotragus lervia*). Sightings of aoudad sheep have increased in recent years to the point where 18 animals were observed along the Devils river in 1999 (Figure 20). Mouflon sheep, currently numbering in the low 100's are found mainly around the park's identified Hunt Area number 5. These two sheep species are suspected of coming from local ranches and game farms where the management and stocking of these animals has been a main goal.

Aoudads are native to northern Africa where rough, rocky, barren waterless tracts are their preferred habitats. Mouflon sheep are native to the islands of Corsica and Sardinia (Mungall and Sheffield, 1994). Both these animals are suited for the Amistad area with wide ranging diets consisting of browse, grass, and forbs. It is not known at this time when these animals were introduced into the area, but observational effects of these animals on vegetation has been observed in Hunt Area 5.

Land Use Development Around The Reservoir

Residential Areas

Since the reservoir's impoundment, 17 private housing subdivisions have been developed adjacent to the reservoir, an example of an area of new housing can be seen in Figure 21. Additional subdivisions are being proposed. With the loss of government subsidies for the sheep and goat industry many ranches are being subdivided into smaller acreages. All of the houses in these subdivisions have septic tanks. Many houses are located on the boundary of the NRA with houses just above the reservoir. Undoubtedly nutrients and other organic materials are leaching through the limestone into the reservoir from these developments.

Val Verde County had 38,721 residents in 1990, while Del Rio, the county seat, had 30,705 (U.S. Census Bureau, 2001). From 1990 to 2000, Val Verde County's population grew 15.8% to 44,856 residents (U.S. Census Bureau, 2001).

In 1971, the 62nd Texas State Legislature passed the Val Verde County Zoning and Building Regulations, which specifically addressed development around Amistad NRA. In 1987, the 70th Texas State Legislature in Chapter 149, Subchapter C. Zoning Near Amistad Recreation Area, Section 1 Section 231.031 through Section 231.072 reiterated the requirements of the regulation and required Val Verde county government to establish an Amistad Zoning Commission under the County Commissioners Court to regulate development within the established zone.

The Zoning Commission has been active in ensuring development meets the scope and intent of the regulations.

Figure 21. Scattered New Residences Along the Devils River.

Trash

Like almost every other public use area in the United States, trash associated with boating use and especially overnight camping with houseboats and small boats is a very real problem.

In popular backcountry boat camping areas, such as the Devils River and the Pecos River, Rangers have spent countless hours collecting, bagging, and removing trash left behind by visitors. Trash that is left over night quickly becomes a target for animals like raccoons and foxes. Once trash is no longer contained, winds quickly spread it around with much of it inevitably ending up in the lake.

The effect this has on aesthetics is quickly evident when checking popular camping sites around the lake. To what degree water quality is affected is unknown.

Trash management at developed areas of the park are based on the use of trash cans and dumpsters. The removal of garbage from all developed areas is accomplished by contract. The following information details the amount of garbage removed from each area weekly.

Governor's Landing	11.8 cubic yards (9 cubic meters)
Diablo East	23.5 cubic yards (18 cubic meters)
Pecos	2.6 cubic yards (2 cubic meters)
Rough Canyon	2.6 cubic yards (2 cubic meters)
San Pedro	6.5 cubic yards (5 cubic meters)
277 North	11.8 cubic yards (9 cubic meters)

Adjacent Oil & Gas Operations

Few economic subsurface mineral deposits are present in the area surrounding the Amistad Reservoir. Exploring for oil and gas has resulted in dry holes, and there appears to be very little potential for successful production locally. Even the production of coal bed methane gas, which has some regional prospects, appears only minimally possible surrounding Amistad and Del Rio, because of the lack of substantial coal beds. Some of the nearest productive coal bed methane deposits along the Rio Grande River appear in the Eagle Pass area 100 miles (161 km) downstream of Amistad Reservoir.

Edwards carbonaceous deposits are common to the Amistad area. Although these deposits can yield substantial oil deposits elsewhere, they are not present locally due to the extensive water presence in the Edwards in this area. Oil and gas are found further north of Amistad Reservoir, where portions of the Edwards deposits lack water (pers. communication with Lisa Norby, NPS Geologic Resource Division, November 15, 2000).

Dryden Hazardous Waste Landfill

In recent years, proposals were submitted for construction of at least three hazardous waste landfills in rural communities along the Texas-Mexico border. One in particular, a hazardous waste landfill near Dryden in Terrell County, has the potential to impact water quality in the Rio Grande Wild and Scenic River and Amistad NRA. The site of the proposed landfill is located approximately 16 miles (26 km) hydraulically up gradient (the route that groundwater travels) and 40 miles (64 km) via surface water drainages from the Rio Grande which flows into Amistad Reservoir. Also, the site is located about 60 miles (97 km) from the Class I protected airshed of Big Bend National Park. In September of 1991, Chemical Waste Management, Inc. (ChemWaste) submitted a 12 volume permit application for disposal of hazardous wastes to the Texas Water Commission (now a part of TNRCC) (Intera, 1991). In addition, ChemWaste submitted a permit application for disposal of Polychlorinated Biphenyls (PCBs) to the USEPA. The applications and technical studies supporting the applications reportedly cost ChemWaste approximately 20 million dollars. Amistad NRA requested assistance from the NPS Water Resources Division and Southwest Regional Office to review the permit applications, participate in meetings involving officials and technical experts representing the applicant and parties opposed to the landfill, and develop technical specifications to assess potential impacts to NPS resources. Groundwater experts from the USGS in Texas provided additional assistance to the park on the landfill issue. Eventually, the Department of the Interior Solicitors Office and State Department became involved in the issue.

Initially, the landfill application met only moderate opposition from the local area. The promise of local jobs and reported facility safety seemed to appease many until it became clear that many unknowns existed regarding the suitability of the site for a landfill and the types of hazardous materials that would be disposed there. The Dryden facility would receive and manage virtually all types of hazardous and non-hazardous wastes, including most of the hazardous wastes identified and listed in 40 CFR Part 261 (Jones and Neuse, Inc., 1991). Incoming wastes may require treatment or processing on site before final disposition. The landfill pit would be lined with multiple clay and synthetic layers with monitor wells on one side only. Initially, no provision was included in the permit application for off-site monitoring. Of primary concern was the fact that the site and surrounding area are underlain by a fractured, carbonate/karst geologic formation that contains several faults or lineaments. Some local experts believe the site was located over a paleokarst collapse feature (Clark, 1993). In addition, little was known about groundwater quality and movement near the site, and the source of nearby springs and seeps. The depth to groundwater at the site is approximately 600 feet (183 m) (Intera, 1992). Groundwater under the site is part of the Edwards-Trinity Aquifer (Rees and Buckner, 1980). The Edwards-Trinity Aquifer is the major source of drinking water for most of south-central Texas. In 1992 and 1993, the cities of Del Rio and Dryden, Cuidad Acuna in Mexico, and local ranchers and farmers began to express concern about the proposed Dryden Landfill.

The NPS was given party status in the permit application process, and proceeded to open a dialog with ChemWaste and the State of Texas in a direct attempt to resolve concerns expressed by local experts. It was determined that groundwater from the Dryden Landfill site would probably flow toward the Rio Grande within the Wild and Scenic River. Surface water draining the site flows toward Lozier Canyon, which drains into the Rio Grande, also within the Wild and Scenic River. Some parties believed the site was located on an active lineament with solution cavities that would facilitate rapid movement of groundwater to the river. Another concern was the risk of accidents along the proposed transportation corridors to the landfill. Ultimately, the NPS with advice from the USGS, requested that the State require ChemWaste to obtain more information about the hydrogeologic features of the area, incorporate an early warning system using off-site monitoring, and incorporate measures to minimize the potential for contamination from spills. At the same time, the NPS attempted to negotiate a settlement agreement with ChemWaste to address groundwater concerns between the site and the Rio Grande (ChemWaste, 1993). The scope of work for the settlement agreement contained two phases. Phase I would consist of a well inventory, water level measurements and a water-level map, and water quality sampling in wells and springs. Phase II would consist of long-term monitoring of selected wells. The settlement agreement was never signed. In November of 1993, the NPS Southwest Regional Director sent a letter to the TNRCC stating NPS concerns, but not opposing nor supporting the project (NPS, 1993).

TNRCC issued two technical notices of deficiency related to the Dryden Landfill permit application during 1992 and 1993. The TNRCC Office of Air Quality issued a notice of deficiency pertaining to the air quality portion of the application in 1993. In 1994, several things occurred which brought the Dryden Landfill issue to a close temporarily. First, the EPA wrote TNRCC expressing its reservations about the facility. Then, the Federal Government of Mexico sent a Diplomatic Note to the United States Government demanding that the United States halt plans for all three hazardous waste dumps in Texas near the United States-Mexican border. Soon after, the Executive Director of the TNRCC ruled that they would no longer review the application and would not issue a draft permit because ChemWaste did not provide complete and/or adequate responses to the TNRCC's staff notices of deficiency. Lastly, the EPA sent ChemWaste a letter identifying 10 deficiencies in the Dryden Landfill permit application. The EPA comments focused on groundwater monitoring requirements and studies necessary before the application can be determined complete. EPA said that if ChemWaste did not respond they would return the application. As a result, ChemWaste chose to withdraw both the hazardous waste application before TNRCC and the PCB application before the EPA. ChemWaste asked the TNRCC to withdraw their application without prejudice, which means they reserve the right to refile at a later date.

Effects of Burning Around the Reservoir

Burning the vegetation adjacent to the reservoir would have very little effect on the water quality. Immediately after a burn, nutrients are released on site, causing grasses to resprout within days. Increased grass growth takes up the available nutrients, thereby reducing the flow of nutrients into the reservoir. Ash falling into the lake during a burn would add phosphorus, however the quantity would be too small to have an effect on aquatic plants or other organisms.

Burning of garbage and landfills could add toxins to the lake from atmospheric deposition. Mercury and eight other metals associated with industrial sources and burning solid waste are increasing in Amistad Reservoir, possibly due to air pollution (Van Metre, et al, 1997). The Ciudad Acuna landfill is burned periodically; the smoke is blown over the reservoir when winds are from the south and southeast, as is common during the spring and summer months.

Effects of Grazing

Grazing at Amistad NRA has been in existence since the formation of the park. The enabling legislation for the park has no mention of grazing. Amistad NRA manages 17 grazing leases located from the park boundary at 1,144.3 feet to 1,124 feet (348.5 m to 342.6 m) elevation. The 17 leases total approximately 6,193 acres (2506 hectares). Lease holders are required to fence grazing areas to existing reservoir water levels. Water levels at Amistad Reservoir have fluctuated between low water levels at 1,058 feet (322.5) to high levels at 1,135 feet (346.0 m). At the conservation pool of 1,117 feet (340.5 m), grazing acreage occupies approximately 15,000 acres (6072 hectares). Spanish goats, sheep, horses and cattle are grazed in the lease areas. Cattle are grazed seasonally in the winter and horses are usually found in small numbers. Goats and sheep can be found in large numbers throughout the lease areas. Herds ranging over 100 animals have been documented along the shoreline.

Grazing effects from livestock are commonly observed along shoreline areas where social trails form to water. Grazing lines on trees and non-vegetated areas are the main effects of large concentrations of animals on park lands. Many livestock trails cross archeological sites and cause compaction and, at times, increase erosion. Dense vegetation growth along the shoreline edge of the reservoir concentrates grazing on park lands. Most grazing occurs below the conservation pool elevation of 1117 feet (340.5 m). Grazing of goats in many areas has reduced the level of salt cedar infestation. This can be observed along the Pecos River and Devils River.

Hazardous Material Transport / Spill Contingency Planning

There is potential for both petroleum and hazardous material spills in the vicinity of the International Amistad Reservoir. US 90, a major east-west thoroughfare, parallels the reservoir along most of its length, crossing the reservoir at three locations: Governor's Landing, Evans Creek, and the Pecos River Arm. The Union Pacific Railroad also has a major rail line which generally parallels US 90 crossing the reservoir at both Governor's Landing and at the Pecos High Bridge (Figure 22). US 277/377, a north-south artery connecting Mexico with Interstate 10 crosses the reservoir via a bridge in the vicinity of San Pedro Canyon. A major petroleum or hazardous materials spill at any of these crossings or along drainages tributary to the reservoir has potential to adversely affect the waters within Amistad NRA. Response to third-party spills at these locations would likely come from Val Verde County Emergency Services, the Texas Highway Patrol, the TNRCC, and/or the Union Pacific Railroad.

Figure 22. Railroad and Hwy 90 Bridges Crossing Amistad Reservoir

Figure 23. Riparian Area and Wetlands Along the Rio Grande Below Amistad Dam.

There are also three marinas providing fuelling services within Amistad NRA. These facilities include NPS and United States Air Force marinas in the vicinity of Diablo East and a NPS marina at Rough Canyon. While Amistad NRA does not have a current spill response contingency plan it does hold a small inventory of spill response equipment and maintains mutual response agreements with both Val Verde County and the United States Air Force pertaining to spill response (Todd Brindle, Amistad NRA, pers. comm., 2000).

Based upon a moderate potential for a spill or other release of a potentially toxic or hazardous substance, it is recommended that Amistad NRA develop a Spill Prevention Control and Countermeasure Plan (SPCC). Such a plan would provide a description of contingency actions to be performed in the event of a spill or release including:

- actions to secure the area to protect the public;
- notification of appropriate agencies in the event of a spill or release;
- spill containment actions including necessary equipment;
- cleanup /removal procedures and equipment.

Assistance in the development of an adequate SPCC Plan can be provided by both the TNRCC's Emergency Response Unit or the Environmental Response, Planning and Assessment Unit of the NPS Environmental Quality Division.

Riparian Zones of Amistad NRA

Amistad NRA contains non-inundated riparian resources along the Rio Grande, Pecos River and the Devils River. These areas contain vegetation communities characteristic of the southwest. High occurrences of salt cedar, willow, river cane, hackberry (*Celtis spp*), huisache (*Acacia farnesiana*), and mesquite (*Prosopis glandulosa*). The riparian resources at Amistad NRA support a high diversity of bird species and provide for migration corridors.

Below the Amistad Dam, the park manages three miles (4.8 km) of riparian zone, occupying approximately 140 acres (56.7 hectares) along the Rio Grande (Figure 23). In the past, a public campground was managed along the river in this area. It was closed in the 1970's with concerns over visitor safety and the security of the Amistad dam. This area of the park contains a study project to monitor the health of bird populations. The IBWC drives the access road to the weir dam, three miles (4.8 km) downstream from the dam, to measure water flows. Water releases from IBWC are the largest influence upon the riparian zone. Large volumes of water have been released in the past, which have infrequently inundated sections of this area for short periods. No permanent effects from these short flood events have been documented. Deposit of sediment in the area may be beneficial to the area.

The Border Patrol conducts monitoring of border activities in a number of the riparian areas found along the Rio Grande. Air boats are used from the Pecos River confluence with the Rio Grande up to the upper limits of the park below Foster crossing. Wave action and frequent boat travel effects on riparian vegetation is unknown at this time. The Border Patrol also drives the three miles (4.8 km) of dirt road below the dam to monitor the boundary.

Springs And Wetlands

The springs around Amistad Reservoir are a popular visitor attraction. Springs in this region have been known to harbor endemic species found no where else, such as the Amistad gambusia (now extinct) which lived in Goodenough Spring prior to reservoir construction. Many of the springs have been inundated during past high lake levels, possibly eliminating endemic species. However, for those springs above conservation pool, It is possible that rare or unique species are still present.

Human and livestock use of springs may be introducing nutrients and exotic species that are altering these ecosystems. Documenting the existing flora and fauna at these springs, in addition to water flow and chemistry would provide a basis for periodic monitoring to determine if springs are being adversely affected.

Reservoir Siltation

Sedimentation rates between 1969 and 1994 were 17.8 inches/year (45cm/yr) or a total of 39.3 feet (12 m) of sediment was deposited in the Rio Grande channel in the lower part of Amistad Reservoir during that 25 year period (Van Metre et al, 1997). This is a very high sedimentation rate compared to other United States reservoirs (Van Metre et al, 1997). As expected, sediment is being deposited where the Rio Grande and the Pecos Rivers flow into the reservoir. The upper Rio Grande Arm and the Pecos River channel are being filled in with sediment. Currently, this has created two major access problems. Cane and other vegetation has grown on the shallow water, narrowing the channel from the Pecos boat ramp to the main part of the reservoir. As a result, only small boats are able to use this access, severely limiting the access to the upper end of the reservoir. A popular visitor attraction is Panther Cave, which is becoming more difficult to access due to the sedimentation along the shoreline. In the future, the rapid rate of sedimentation will likely create additional problems with Amistad NRA facilities.

Recreational Issues Related to Water Resources

Swim Beach Water Quality Monitoring

The Amistad Reservoir is designated as Segment 2305 of the Rio Grande Basin by the TNRCC . The designated water uses for this segment include contact recreation, high aquatic life, and public water supply (TNRCC, 2000).

Historically, there have been four designated (though unguarded) recreational swimming beaches within Amistad NRA. These include the Governor's Landing, Viewpoint Cliffs, and the Old Dam Site along the Rio Grande arm of the reservoir as well as Rough Canyon in the Devils River arm (NPS, 1999a). However, lowered water levels over the last several years have made three of these sites inaccessible and Governor's Landing in the Diablo East area of the National Recreation Area is the only currently usable swimming beach (Todd Brindle, Amistad NRA, pers. comm., 2000).

The final draft of the 2000 Texas Clean Water Act Section 303(d) list of impaired waters does not indicate any known water quality problems within the International Amistad Reservoir (Segment 2305) (TNRCC, 2000). However, NPS Director's Order 83: Public Health (dated August 2, 1999) directs NPS park managers to reduce the risk of waterborne disease by requiring that designated bathing beaches, and other heavily utilized recreational waters, be appropriately monitored for bacterial indicators of water borne pathogens. Guidance pertaining to this monitoring are found in Reference Manual 83 (NPS, 1999b) and include:

- Conducting a sanitary survey
- Preparing a bathing beach monitoring protocol
- Sampling for *Escherichia coli* bacteria levels
- Issuing swimming advisories when bathing beach waters exceed the bacterial standards

Amistad NRA initiated a recreational water quality monitoring screening program in August, 2000 (Todd Brindle, Amistad NRA, pers. comm., 2000). This program consists of weekly monitoring of one site at the only currently accessible swimming beach (Governor's Landing) for fecal coliform bacteria, *E. coli*, and enterococci bacteria. Samples are collected by park staff and sent for analyses by the San Antonio River Authority. Because of the distances involved, the samples exceed the recommended 8 hour holding time, but the analysis are considered to be acceptable for general beach monitoring purposes (Chuck Lorea, San Antonio River Authority, pers. com., 2000).

Data collected for August and September, 2000 for the Governor's Landing Beach are presented in Table 12. These data indicate that fecal coliform, *E. coli*, and enterococci bacteria levels fall well below the recommended maximum limits for contact recreation (geometric means of 200 for fecal coliform; 126 for *E. coli*; and 33 for enterococci), though the bacterial levels in September were slightly elevated from levels found in August possibly due to the natural, seasonal decrease in ultra violet radiation during the latter month.

Public health and safety considerations suggest that Amistad NRA continue their beach monitoring program, expanding it, if necessary, to include other designated beaches when water levels rise to where these beaches are again accessible for public use.

Table 12. Recreational Water Quality Monitoring Results at Governor's Landing Beach for 1999-2000.

AUGUST 2000	08/01/00	08/08/00	08/22/00	08/28/00
fecal coliform (per 100 mL)		3	9	12
E. coli (per 100 mL)		<1	9	12
Enterococci (per 100 mL)	<9	1	5	<1
SEPTEMBER 2000	09/05/00	09/13/00	09/18/00	09/26/00
fecal coliform (per 100 mL)	2	6	24	38
E. coli (per 100 mL)	2	<1	24	10
Enterococci (per 100 mL)	<1	<1	12	22

(Information from Juan Gonzalez, Amistad NRA)

Effects of Fish Cleaning on Water Quality

Fish cleaning has no negative effect on water quality because the majority of the fish guts, heads, tails, and skins left over from fish caught in the reservoir are not put back into the reservoir.

From 1970 to 1980, fishermen actively caught fish and cleaned them along the shoreline. In about 1980, the NPS began building "fish cleaning stations" at the major boat ramps. One fish cleaning station was built at the Diablo East boat ramp. A second fish cleaning station was built at the second most popular boat ramp, the Rough Canyon boat ramp, on the upper Devils River arm of the reservoir. In 1985, a third fish cleaning station was built at the Pecos River boat ramp.

These fish cleaning stations were extremely popular, and probably about 80% of the fish caught on the reservoir since 1985 were cleaned at these stations. Many fish not cleaned at these fish cleaning stations were cleaned somewhere other than the reservoir shoreline. Several local commercial campgrounds have their own fish cleaning stations as a courtesy to their campers. Some local people prefer to clean their fish at their homes. Some fishermen release their fish alive back into the reservoir.

The fish cleaning stations are comprised of an industrial-strength garbage disposal surrounded by kitchen-style cutting boards. Hand-activated shower-type water nozzles are suspended from the ceiling. Electrical plug-ins are provided for those fishermen preferring to use an electric cutting knife. The fish are cleaned and filleted on the cutting boards, and the fish guts, head, tail, and skin are deposited in the garbage disposal in the center. A button activates the grinder, and the ground-up fish effluent pass through a pipe to an underground holding tank adjacent to the fish cleaning station. Periodically, NPS Maintenance presonnel pump out the accumulated fish effluent with a vacuum truck, and deposit the material in sewage lagoons located adjacent to the Amistad Dam. At no time was this fish effluent ever dumped into the lake. This fish effluent therefore had no negative impact on water quality at the reservoir. Since most people preferred to use these convenient fish cleaning stations, the end result has been a dramatic reduction in the potential quantity of fish guts, heads, and tails that were placed directly into the reservoir by fishermen. Beginning in 1999, the fish effluent in the fish cleaning station holding tanks was no longer placed in the sewage lagoons by Amistad Dam. Instead, this fish effluent is transported by vacuum truck to a fish effluent drying bed located in the park. The material is allowed to dry out, then is collected and transported to the local landfill.

Effects of bass tournaments on water quality

Bass tournaments appear to have little negative impact on water quality at Amistad Reservoir.

Amistad Reservoir has had primarily large-mouth bass fishing tournaments since initial inundation in 1969. The first major tournament, comprised of approximately 500 bass boats, occurred at the reservoir in the early 1970's. Most bass tournaments are much smaller however, and are comprised of 15 to 30 boats each. There are perhaps four tournaments per year with more than 200 boats. There is usually one tournament per year that has 350 to 500 boats entered. On most spring, summer, and fall week-ends, there are probably three to eight separate bass tournaments taking place at Amistad Reservoir, with a total number of participating boats ranging from 50 to 200. The largest recorded bass tournament at Amistad Reservoir was the Travis Open Bass Tournament in September of 1998, when there were 596 boats entered.

The bass tournament activity could potentially cause minimal negative impacts to water quality for several different reasons:

- Pollutants put into the lake as a result of outboard motors (see oil and gas contamination section below).
- Chemicals from the "live-wells" in the bass boats, where the fish are kept alive until they are weighed at the end of the tournament day
- During warm water periods (August and September), studies have shown that up to 65% of the fish released alive from the tournament weigh-ins die after five to eight days. That could calculate to 80 to 600 fish per week-end (depending on number and size of bass tournaments that week-end) dying and rotting in the reservoir five to eight days after release during these warm-water periods.

A number of methods are used to reduce mortality levels on fish during tournaments. Livewell additives are used to replace the slime removed from the skin of fish during handling. The loss of this slime protection, in conjunction with warm water temperatures, causes the rapid growth of fungus that weakens the fish over a period of four to eight days, then secondary infections can cause death. Texas Parks and Wildlife Department Inland Fisheries Division recommends using a salt bath for the control of fungus during tournament releases (Jimmy Dean, TPWD, pers. comm., 2001). Once fish have been weighed, they are dipped in a salt bath solution, and then released. Other procedures for reducing the mortality of bass during summer tournaments is to add oxygen and ice to the livewells while fishing. The effects of livewell water additives on water quality in the reservoir is unknown at this time. Most livewells are emptied after boats have been trailored, thus reducing the chance of contaminating reservoir waters.

SCUBA Diving (submerged hazards)

Amistad Reservoir is a very popular dive site. Many dive operations from the surrounding area come to do open water training. Amistad Reservoir is popular with sport divers because of its good visibility. Diving can be dangerous however if the diver is not well trained or does not follow safety procedures.

One noted submerged hazard is the old Devils River dam. The top of the dam is under about 30 feet (9 m) of water. The dam is off limits to divers after a diver fatality. A diver entered the old control structure and could not find his way out. The structure has a heavy silt deposit and divers can lose visibility and become disoriented.

The lake has many cave and rock shelters under water. Cave diving requires special skills and training and can be very dangerous to an inexperienced diver. Some divers enter the rock shelters without knowing they are there. The first sign is the loss of light. The diver can become disoriented and even claustrophobic. The danger is multiplied if they do not maintain bottom control and stir up the silt.

The major recreation use of the lake is fishing and this leads to another hazard; snagged and broken fishing line. Many of the new fishing lines have a very high breaking strength. A well-trained diver that might become tangled would use a dive knife to cut loose from the entanglement. If the diver does not remain calm this situation can be fatal. There has been one diver who became entangled in 80 feet (24 m) of water. He was properly equipped but his training and experience level was not sufficient for conditions. Park divers recovered the diver's body three days later after an extensive search. Some old ranch fences still remain under water and can pose an entanglement threat. Unlike the fishing line they are easier to see and less of an entanglement risk.

The lake has some very deep areas, which can be a hazard if the diver stays too long, due to decompression problems. There is no local hyperbaric chamber used to treat decompression problems, the closest being in San Antonio which is 3 hours away.

Marina Operations and Maintenance

Refueling of Boats

There are three authorized marina operations on the reservoir. Each marina provides boat rental service, slip and dock rental and on the water fuel service. All marinas have automatic fuel flow detectors and shut off valves as well as manual shut off valves. Emergency kill switches are located adjacent to all fuel areas. Fire suppression and spill containment materials are readily available on all fuel docks. All marinas have an Emergency Operations Plan for fuel spill and other contaminants. All staff are trained in spill prevention and mitigation. In the last five years, four spills occurred from broken gas lines and spills at the pumps.

The Rough Canyon Marina has one fuel dock, which has a single fuel pump. It supplies 89 octane, mid grade fuel to boaters. The marina also has two other land based fuel pumps offering 89 and 93 octane, mid-grade and premium fuels. The fuel is supplied from an above ground tank with a capacity for 1500 gallons (5,670 liters) of mid-grade and 500 gallons (1,890 liters) of premium fuel, total capacity being 2000 gallons (7,569 liters). Future plans call for an additional tank supplying diesel fuel for the land based pumps. The fuel, equipment, and maintenance is supplied by Pico Petroleum Products (Diamond Shamrock brand fuel).

The fuel is supplied to the fuel dock via a partial underground pipe and a partial above ground flexible fuel line. There are two cut off valves at the fuel tank and four additional cut offs going down to the fuel dock. The fuel dock has two fire extinguishers and is illuminated at night by a pole mounted, land based lighting system. In 1986 the flexible fuel line broke resulting in 20 gallons (76 liters) or less of fuel entering the lake.

The marina also has a dock with 32 boat slips as well as 17 mooring buoys and eight rental boats. The marina maintains the docks while Pico/Diamond Shamrock maintains the fuel tanks, pumps, lines and fuel equipment. The marina also responds to any emergencies pertaining to moored or docked boats that are under their care.

The Southwind Marina is operated by the Laughlin Air Force Base in Del Rio. The marina operates two fuel tanks. One tank, 300 gallons (1,134 liters) is located in the maintenance area of the development and is used for support equipment. The second fuel tank is located near the parking lot and holds 2,000 gallons (7,569 liters). This tank has three safety cut-off valves and is used for boats only. The fuel dock has two pumps. There are 56 boat slips and 27 boat rentals. Boat rentals average about 300 per year. There has been two gasoline spills in the last five years at this dock. One 15 gallon (57 liters) spill occurred on land, from a broken line connection. The dirt was removed and hauled out of the area. The second spill on the gas dock involved 5 gallons (19 liters) from a broken hose. Absorbent devices were used to remove the fuel from the lake.

The Amistad Reservoir Resort and Marina is found at the Diablo East developed area. The marina contains 52 boat slips. There is one 6,000 gallon (22,680 liters) fuel tank, which is divided into two compartments. This tank was installed in 1999 and contains one compartment, which holds 4,000 gallons (15,120 liters) of unleaded fuel. The other compartment holds 2,000 gallons (7,569 liters) of pre-mix fuel. The tank is above ground and marked as fuel and has a chain link fence protecting it. There are six cutoff valves for this tank. There are 10 house boat rentals that occur at this marina. Length of boats are 56 to 59 feet (17 to 18 m). The houseboats are self contained and store all gray water and human waste in tanks found inside the boats. One houseboat pumpout station with a 20 gallon (76 liter) holding tank is used at the marina. This is connected directly into the sewer system at Diablo East. During 1999, house boat rentals totaled 338 use events. Ten small boats are rented from this marina (length 12 feet to 26 feet long) (3.6 to 8 m long). During 1999, motor boat rentals totaled 29 use events. The fuel pump dock has two pumps, one for regular gas and the other for pre-mix gas.

Oil and Gas Contamination

The effects of oil and gas contamination on water quality are present, but to what degree are unknown at this time. The principal sources of oil and gas contamination at Amistad Reservoir are (1) the use of 2 cycle outboard motors and (2) on the water refueling at two marinas as described above.

Emissions from two cycle motors, in which the oil is mixed with the fuel, often produces a sheen on the water. This is readily observed when boats are started and idled in calm water conditions. It is unknown if any studies at Amistad Reservoir have addressed this issue or if the level of contamination is even measurable with current levels of use. This effect is most noticeable when there are heavy concentrations of boats in protected areas such as the Diablo East and Rough Canyon harbors at peak use periods. Greater amounts of contamination are probably emitted when boats are operating at higher speeds, but those effects would be more dispersed and not as noticeable.

Personal WaterCraft (PWC) use at Amistad NRA is somewhat limited at this time in comparison to fishing or other recreational uses. PWC use is on the increase and impacts from this will likely increase in the future.

Recently, a common gasoline additive has been found to have health risks, methyl tertiary butyl ether (MTBE). Currently, TNRCC is collecting samples statewide to determine which water bodies and wells have detectable concentrations of this chemical compound. At Amistad NRA, areas around marina fuel docks, and near underground storage tanks would have the greatest risk of contamination.

Human Waste/Gray Water

Amistad Reservoir water quality is affected by human waste from camping and gray water from camping and house boating.

Camping activities on the shorelines of Amistad Reservoir produce noticeable amounts of human waste in certain areas of the reservoir. Two heavily impacted areas are popular campsites on the Devils and Pecos River arms of the reservoir. From 1973 through 1994, heavy camping use on the Pecos River produced heavy undesirable impacts to the limited numbers of campsites available. Almost every suitable campsite, those riverbank areas with soil and vegetation for wind breaks and privacy, had at least one, and in some cases several, visitor created, pit toilets. These usually consisted of a shallow hole or trench in the ground with a wooden frame and attached toilet seat placed over the hole. Fluctuating lake levels would occasionally place many of these toilets under water. NPS employees spent many weekends during the early 1990's removing these makeshift toilets. Low water levels beginning in the mid 1990's greatly limited access to the sites and stopped this heavy use. Higher reservoir water levels will allow access to these sites.

Similar conditions will also be found on the Devils River arm of the lake and to a lesser degree in the Cow Creek area. In other backcountry areas of the park this has not been a noticeable problem primarily due to the wider disbursement of campers. Increased backcountry camping without more strict waste management regulations will most likely cause this problem to intensify.

Human waste problems have not generally been associated with houseboats due to the use of approved marine sanitation devices. Human waste problems in front country areas have also not contributed significantly to water quality problems because of the park's ability to place portable toilet facilities at problem locations with little advance notice and to construct suitable toilets.

Water quality problems with gray water from boat campers and houseboats have traditionally been perceived as less of a problem. Houseboats do put a significant amount of gray water into the lake. However, it is usually not concentrated in specific areas. Increases in camping could make this more of a problem in the future.

In 1999, Amistad NRA completed the installation of 32 vault toilets throughout developed areas of the park, which include campgrounds, parking lots and boatramps. These toilets were installed to reduce maintenance issues with chemical toilets and also to further the lifetime of use between pumping of the vaults. The estimated pumpout for these toilets are estimated at three-year intervals. There are 5 to 6 chemical toilets used at the park to deal with special activities or where human waste issues arise for short periods.

Amistad NRA Facilities Issues

National Park Service Water Supply

Potable water supply provided by wells appears adequate at this time for Amistad NRA, and appears to be adequate at this time for fire fighting purposes.

Water distribution is not optimal to all facilities at this time but is believed sufficient by park staff. The concession operated store at Diablo East has access to potable water through temporary hoses only. Permanent plumbing would require wastewater connections and a lift station to complete the installation. There are no current plans for this construction. A new boat ramp development at Box Canyon may need potable water in the future. The Pecos River site has periodically been challenged to meet visitor's potable water demands. However this demand has occurred only when the reservoir is near full and the visitor use is high at the site. For more than five years, the visitor use of the site has been sparse because of low water conditions. Water supply issues at Pecos River site may be re-evaluated in the future if the water level and site visitation return to their previous condition.

Table 13. Potable Water Supply Wells serving Amistad NRA.

Well Name/Location	Developed Depth (feet)	Storage (X 1000 Gallons)
Governor's Landing	390	.250 (Pressure. Tank)
Diablo East	490	250
Rough Canyon	520	27
Pecos River	625	25
Headquarters	400	N/A

Information provided by Amistad NRA staff.

Wastewater System

Sanitary wastewater is collected and treated using septic tanks with evaporation transpiration beds. Sludge collected from the septic tanks is dried in the beds and later disposed of locally in a sanitary landfill.

Some of the wastewater collection piping and pumping infrastructure is approaching or older than its design age and may require replacement in years to come. Portions of the collection system above ground or the water are particularly vulnerable to age, sun, or vandalism-caused breakage.

Major portions of the wastewater system at Diablo East were recently rehabilitated, but the pump out and wet well holding tank for the houseboat system has breakage and capacity constraints. Portions of this site's lift stations and piping are scheduled for repairs in the immediate future.

The evaporation beds for the wastewater sludge at Pecos River are adequate in capacity during most use conditions, but can overflow during extreme rainfall conditions. The park should evaluate options for decreasing the risk of this condition.

Sludge from the Headquarters and Diablo East wastewater systems goes to a drying area at Hunt Area 2 along with fish processing waste. The resultant dried sludge is properly disposed of in the local landfill.

Vault Toilets are used by the public at Box Canyon, while chemical toilets are used at Governor's Landing. A septic system serves the Governor's Landing VIP site. A dump station for recreation vehicles is provided at Diablo East.

On the lake, two locations are provided for pumping out visitor or staff boat wastewater holding tanks.

Tire Breakwater

Floating tire breakwaters are used to protect the boat marina facilities at Diablo East and Air Force marinas. The connected floating tires disperse wind and boat wake caused wave action. Concern has been voiced by staff and visitors about the potential impacts to water quality from the tires being in contact with the water, and in exposure to sun and wave action for many years. No actual testing has occurred at Amistad for any potential effects, and very few references were uncovered that dealt directly with tires in aquatic systems.

Scientists with the United States Bureau of Reclamation's Environmental Sciences Section and their Lower Colorado Regional Office investigated potential toxicity effects of tire breakwaters and artificial reef systems constructed of tires in freshwater reservoirs. Using freshly cut rubber plugs from tires and whole tires, tire leachate was extracted and tested for chemical constituents and to determine actual effects upon several fish species. Test water was collected from Lake Mead, Nevada and had a pH range of 8.4 to 8.6. High levels of copper, lead, cadmium, and zinc were found, but the tests confirmed that the toxicity to the fish was caused primarily by the extracted zinc. However, the quantity of leachate derived from the tire material in the reservoir water represents a worst case scenario for a very small water volume with a large quantity of tires. Thus, the authors did not believe that the zinc (or other observed metals) would ever cause acute or even chronic toxicity in medium to large reservoir systems having tire breakwaters or artificial reefs constructed with tires (Nelson et al, 1994).

Thus, to the degree that the tires in the floating breakwater disintegrate in the aquatic environment, some quantities of zinc would be slowly released into the reservoir. It is also likely, that individual tires or the entire breakwater could be replaced prior to full disintegration of the tires, as the breakwater would lose its wave dispersing effectiveness. Existing zinc levels in Amistad are above TNRCC screening levels in sediments but not in water samples. If quantities of zinc are not found in high levels in the reservoir water already it is not likely that the small release of zinc from the tires is a major issue. Acidic conditions (pH < 7) would favor faster dissolution of zinc from the tires and pose a higher toxicity potential to aquatic species. However, pH levels in Amistad are normally 7.5 to 8.0, thus there is even a lesser probability of zinc in the tires posing a major issue.

Other materials in the tires are apparently very stable and mostly inert in the aquatic system. Bacterial action would also slowly consume the rubber components in the tires, and that action would be competing with some ultraviolet light and ozone caused breakdown at the water surface. In each of these cases, any zinc releases would again be seen as probably small, and eventually stopped as a disintegrating tire was removed or replaced.

One reference described zinc phytotoxicity in plants grown in weathered or degraded tire augmented soils of neutral to acidic pH. Zinc is used as a filler in rubber tires, but is only released to any large degree when the tires are ground up as compost and soil amendments, burned, or significantly weathered to the point of disintegration (Rufus Chaney, USDA Agricultural Research Service, pers. comm. 2001). Thus, the tires removed eventually from the breakwater should be appropriately disposed of in proper landfill or recycled.

Flood Hazards

The NPS is directed to manage the use of floodplains in accordance with standards and procedures set forth in Executive Order 11988, "Floodplain Management". Agency-specific direction for complying with the Order is provided in Special Directive 93-4, "Floodplain Management Guidelines".

As stated in the Guideline, it is NPS policy to avoid the use of the regulatory floodplain for most types of developments whenever there is a practical alternative. The regulatory floodplain is defined as the 100-year, 500-year, or maximum possible floodplain depending upon the nature of flooding in the area and the type of activity or development. In regions susceptible to flash flooding, where flooding occurs so rapidly that persons cannot become aware of the danger and take necessary precautions within the time available, the maximum floodplain is the regulatory floodplain. In other areas that are not at risk from flash flooding, the type of park activity determines what the regulatory floodplain is. So-called "critical actions" have the 500-year floodplain as the regulatory floodplain. Critical actions include activities with a high degree of human and/or resource risk. Examples include hospitals, museums, large hazardous material storage, etc. A more complete explanation of critical actions can be found in the Guidelines. Other types of actions, for example, most visitor centers, park housing, etc. in non-flash flood areas have the 100-year floodplain as the regulatory floodplain. Some park facilities and functions are exempt from compliance with the Executive Order such as water dependent activities such as boat docks and bridges. Roads and trails are also generally exempt from floodplain compliance.

In the case where there is no practicable non-floodplain location available for an essential park activity, NPS policy may permit development in the regulatory floodplain. In this case, a Statement of Findings (SOF) is prepared. The SOF describes the rationale for why a floodplain location is the only practicable alternative, presents an analysis of the hazard associated with flooding, and describes how flood hazard will be mitigated up to the level of the regulatory flood. The SOF process is ordinarily conducted in concert with the National Environmental Policy Act (NEPA) process.

Hydrologic features in south central Texas in the area around Amistad NRA include Amistad Reservoir itself, major rivers such as the Rio Grande River, Pecos River, and Devils River, many small streams, and numerous ephemeral and intermittent washes. The nature of flooding in each of these types of water courses is quite different, so it follows that safety concerns for park developments differ according to which type of water body is near. Amistad Reservoir water levels change relatively slowly and are most affected by long-term climatic conditions such as protracted drought or wet conditions. The large surface area and storage volume of the reservoir attenuates lake level response to individual storm events. Factors relating to flood hazard associated with high lake levels include long-duration inundation periods with little or no flow velocity and, generally, advance warning time measured in days. Major river systems such as the Rio Grande, respond to large-scale storm events that often occur over a several day period and may occur in areas distant from the NRA. Floods in the large rivers are deep and have high velocity but, in this region, are generally confined within the canyon walls. These floods can last for several days and generally have warning time of at least several hours and often much more. Smaller streams in the Amistad area can respond dramatically to brief intense rainfall events that most often occur over small areas close to the area of flooding. The high velocity and sudden, unpredictable nature of these floods make them very hazardous. Additionally, floods in smaller drainages tend to interact more with roads and bridges and therefore, may present more threat to humans.

In general, park activities that are located along the major rivers or the reservoir should be considered as having regulatory floodplain of either the 100- or 500-year flood depending upon whether the activity is considered a critical action. Park developments near flash flood prone washes and small streams may be in high hazard locations and therefore, are required to be out of (or protected against) the maximum possible flood. Most park infrastructure in Amistad NRA is found above the maximum 1,144.3 foot (348.8 m) reservoir water level as required by park legislation (NPS, 1987). The designated 100-year flood level for the reservoir, assuming a starting flood level of 1,117 feet (340.5 m), is set at 1,140.4 feet (347.6 m). A development zone was created for Amistad NRA that requires all significant developments except boat launch ramps to be above 1,144.3 feet (348.8 m). Minor developments for visitor use provided below 1,140 feet (347.6 m), such as unpaved roads, picnic areas, swim beaches, and primitive campgrounds, will be designed to withstand occasional temporary flooding (NPS, 1987). Boat launch facilities, certain roads, and some day use facilities are in floodplain locations and are considered to be excepted actions with respect to floodplain compliance. The biggest threat to minor developments and visitor use occurred in 1974 when the reservoir water level reached 1,135.7 feet (346.2 m), rising over 6 feet (1.8 m) in one day, and then stood above 1,125 (342.6 m)feet through the end of the year. Some developments, such as the Pecos River visitor area, are located on terraces that are relatively high compared to nearby water features. This situation is a result of nearly all stream and river valleys being deeply incised and having very steep valley walls.

It is recognized that risk to humans from flooding does exist at the Amistad NRA, particularly in the small drainages that are most susceptible to flash flooding. Additionally, risk to recreationists using the major river corridors is present for persons unaware or unprepared for high water conditions.

Human risk to flooding is managed at Amistad NRA by providing information to visitors and staff regarding known high water conditions in the rivers and weather conditions conducive to flash floods in the small drainages. General information is provided to visitors informing them of what areas are susceptible to sudden flooding and what to do in case of flooding. The Pecos River is one good example where the river flows through very steep incised canyons. Visitors using this area during heavy rain events are at risk from floods. During such events, Amistad NRA informs the public on flood stage levels and expected periods of severe rise in river water flow.

Fisheries Issues

Many complex fisheries issues have been discussed as part of the on-going work on the Fisheries Management Plan for Amistad NRA. That plan will discuss all these issues in detail and is expected to be completed by the end of 2001.

Threatened/Endangered Species and Species of Conservation Concern

A number of fish species native to the lower Rio Grande in the vicinity of Amistad Reservoir, the lower Pecos River drainage and the Devils River drainage have been extirpated and/or significantly reduced in both range and numbers since the development of the Amistad Dam and Reservoir.

The Rio Grande silvery minnow (Hybognathus amarus) was formerly one of the most widespread and abundant species in the Rio Grande Basin of New Mexico, Texas, and Mexico. However, recent surveys indicate that its range has been reduced by as much as

95% of its original range (currently found only from Cochiti Reservoir downstream to Elephant Butte Reservoir). The silvery minnow was extirpated from the lower Rio Grande in the vicinity of Amistad Reservoir around 1961, probably due to the introduction of non-native species and the construction and operation of the Amistad Reservoir (Bestgen and Platania, 1991).

Additional fish species that have been lost in the vicinity of Amistad NRA include the phantom shiner *(Notropis orca)*, the bluntnose shiner *(Notropis simus)*, the Amistad gambusia *(Gambusia amistadensis)*, and the blotched gambusia *(Gambusia senilis)* (Gary Garrett, TPWD, pers. comm., 2000).

TPWD currently lists 12 fish species as "species of conservation concern" in the Rio Grande/Amistad Reservoir Area. These include:

> American eel *(Anguilla rostrata)*
> Mexican stoneroller *(Campostoma ornatum)*
> Proserpine shiner *(Cyprinella proserpina)*
> Devils River minnow *(Dionda diaboli)*
> Chihuahua shiner *(Notropis chihuahua)*
> Rio Grande shiner *(Notropis jemezanus)*
> Blue sucker *(Cycleptus elongatus)*
> Mexican redhorse *(Scartomyzon austrin)*
> Headwater catfish *(Ictalurus lupus)*
> Chihuahua catfish *(Ictalurus sp.)*
> Conchos pupfish *(Cyprinodon eximius)*
> Rio Grande darter *(Etheostoma grahami)*

The Devils River minnow *(Dionda diaboli)*, found primarily in the channels of fast flowing, spring-fed water over gravel bottoms (Harrell, 1978), was an abundant species in the Devils River, San Felipe Creek and Sycamore Creek of southwest Texas, as recently as the mid-1970s. This species is now a federally listed threatened species (Nathan Allan, USFWS, pers. comm. 2000). In a study of this species conducted in the early 1990s, Garrett et al (1992) reported that this species has shown an alarming decline in both range and relative abundance since the 1970s.

Other Aquatic Biological Resources

Freshwater mussels have suffered a greater decline than any other wide-ranging faunal group in North America (Jennings, 1998). They have recently been recognized as important barometers of environmental quality as they are often among the first organisms to decline when environmental conditions deteriorate (Howells, 1998).

The decline in the range and abundance of the freshwater mussel has been apparent in the Rio Grande drainage where a number of historic freshwater mussel species are thought to have been extirpated. Primary threats to freshwater mussel survival within the Rio Grande basin reflect dramatic habitat loss and alteration. Recent surveys being conducted by the TPWD suggest that only three species of native freshwater mussels probably remain in the vicinity of Amistad NRA including the: Tampico pearlymussel

(Cyrtonaias tampicoensis), the bleufer *(Potamilus purpuratus)*, and the paper pondshell *(Utterbackia imbecillis)* (Robert Howells, TPWD, pers. comm., 2000).

The range and abundance of freshwater mussels within the entire Rio Grande drainage appears to be in decline. In the vicinity of Amistad NRA, limited habitat and fluctuating reservoir water levels are most probably responsible for the decline in the reservoir. Increasing salinity has totally extirpated freshwater mussels in the lower reaches of the Pecos River, and scouring and de-watering may have affected habitat and abundance within the Devils River (Robert Howells, TPWD, pers. comm., 2000).

In addition, the larval phase of the freshwater mussel is dependent upon a fish host. For many mussel species, the fish host is species specific. The fish hosts for the larval Tampico pearlymussel *(Cyrtonacias tampicoensis)* include the long nose gar *(Lepisosteus osseus)*, spotted gar *(Lepisosteus oculatus)*, Rio Grande cichlid *(Cichlasoma cyanoguttatum)*, and golden shiner *(Notemigonus crysoleucas)*; the larval bleufer's *(Potamilus purpuratus)* fish host is the freshwater drum *(Aplodinutus grunniens)*; while the fish hosts for the paper pondshell *(Utterbackia imbecillis)* includes a number of species (Robert Howells, TPWD, pers. comm., 2000).

The TPWD is currently in the final year of a four year study of freshwater mussel populations in the Texas portion of the Rio Grande. Data from this survey will be useful in evaluating the current range and abundance information (Robert Howells, TPWD, pers. comm., 2000).

CONSIDERATIONS FOR FUTURE ACTIONS

The health and quality of the water-related resources form an integral component of the National Park Service mandate at Amistad NRA to provide for public outdoor recreation use and enjoyment of the US portion of the Lake Amistad Reservoir and to protect their scenic, scientific, and cultural values. These resources not only include the reservoir, but also several miles of the 3 rivers that flow into the reservoir, numerous springs and seeps along the rivers and reservoir edge which support highly important aquatic habitat, and the aquatic biological resources which have been significantly altered by the formation of the Lake Amistad Reservoir.

Thus, while the ownership of the water rights within the NRA remain vested with the State of Texas and Government of Mexico, the success of meeting NPS management objectives delineated by the United States Congress in establishing Amistad NRA requires extensive coordination and cooperation among the governments of Mexico and the United States, the states of Coahuila, Chihuahua, and Texas, the International Boundary and Water Commission (IBWC), as well as adjacent landowners and downstream holders of water rights .

Specific issues and recommended actions to be considered for future action include:

♦ **INCREASED PARTICIPATION IN TEXAS CLEAN RIVERS WATER QUALITY MONITORING PROGRAM** -- The IBWC and the Texas Natural Resource Conservation Commission (TNRCC) have recently initiated an impressive cooperative water quality monitoring program with several stations of direct relevance to the status and long term trends of water quality conditions within Amistad NRA.

   RECOMMENDED ACTION: While staffing at Amistad NRA is limited, it is strongly recommended that Amistad NRA take advantage of this program by increasing its participation in the Texas Clean Rivers Water Quality Monitoring Program by becoming a cooperator and assisting with the monthly collection of water quality samples at specified park locations. The NRA should assure that relevant water quality data from the Texas Clean Rivers Water Quality Monitoring Program is captured and utilized by NPS Chihuahuan Desert Network Vital Signs Monitoring Program as one of the important long term indicators of ecosystem health for the NRA. The NRA should further assure that the water quality data are analyzed and shared in such a manner that it can be used in management decision making by the NPS and other agencies charged with the management of Amistad Reservoir. NRA should also explore the possibility of utilizing either Texas Clean Rivers Water Quality Monitoring Program or NPS Vital Signs Monitoring Program as possible sources for expanding long term water quality monitoring on the Devils River, because of the limited amount of information currently available for this important tributary.

♦ **DEVELOP A SPRINGS PROTECTION STRATEGY AND DESIGN AN INVENTORY AND LONG-TERM MONITORING PROGRAM FOR CRITICAL SPRING SITES--** Springs constitute an important water resource at Amistad NRA both by serving as a source of a significant quantity of water entering the reservoir and supporting critical aquatic and riparian habitat types in this arid environment. Discharge, flow patterns, and the water quality of springs are determined largely by rainfall patterns and the complex karstic geology underlying much of the region, but may also be influenced by human-related activities such as land use, ground water withdrawals, changes in reservoir levels, the presence of exotic species, inappropriate visitor use, etc.

RECOMMENDED ACTION: The NRA is encouraged to develop strategy for the long-term protection of spring resources. Initially, a baseline inventory and mapping effort should be completed to locate and quantify attributes associated with the existing springs including spring flow, water chemistry (including isotopic work to determine spring source), aquatic biological resources, and riparian vegetation. Following the initial baseline inventory, a monitoring strategy should be initiated as part of the Chihuahuan Desert Vital Signs Monitoring Program to monitor the long-term status and trends of key (ie "vital sign") indicators relating to this important resource. Assistance in designing inventory and monitoring approaches should be sought from NPS units such as Big Bend National Park and Lake Mead NRA which have existing programs, the Texas District of the USGS Water Resources Division, the Water Resources Division of the NPS, or the NPS Servicewide Inventory and Monitoring Program. Finally, advice in developing a protection strategy for these resources should also be sought from the Water Rights Branch of the NPS Water Resources Division who have considerable experience in developing similar protection strategies in other areas of the NPS.

♦ **SUPPORT THE DEVELOPMENT OF A BI-NATIONAL FISHERIES MANAGEMENT PLAN – There** are a number of complex fisheries issues relevant to the management of the Amistad Reservoir. Today, this reservoir provides an important recreational fishery for Texas and commercial/recreational fishery for Mexico. However, a number of fish species native to the lower Rio Grande, the lower Pecos River, and the Devils River drainage have been extirpated and/or significantly reduced in both range and numbers since the development of Amistad Dam and Reservoir.

RECOMMENDED ACTION: The Secretariat of Agriculture, Livestock, Rural Development, Fisheries, and Nutrition (SAGARPA) in Mexico, along with the Texas Parks and Wildlife Department (TPWD), NPS, and US Fish and Wildlife Service in the United States all have management responsibilities for various aspects of the aquatic resources within the Amistad Reservoir and its surrounding drainages. In January, 2000 SAGARPA, TPWD and the NPS initiated an effort to develop a Bi-national Fisheries Management Plan. Amistad NRA is both a strong advocate and active participant in the development of this plan, which should be completed and submitted for approval to the appropriate management agencies in 2002.

♦ **ENHANCE INTERAGENCY RELATIONSHIPS FOR DEVELOPING RESEARCH PROPOSALS FOCUSSED UPON WATER-RELATED SYNOPTIC RESEARCH STUDIES IDENTIFIED THROUGHOUT THIS SCOPING PROCESS – The** assessment of current studies and needs conducted as part of this water resources scoping report identified several topical areas for which further synoptic research studies were highly desirable. These include needs to better quantify and understand the mechanisms driving increased salinity and mercury deposition in the Amistad Reservoir, the need to evaluate the potential impacts of increasing salinity and chloride concentrations upon aquatic life, the need to perform a multi-seasonal baseline inventory of algal species present in the Amistad Reservoir, the need to develop protocols for sampling and responding to fish kill and algal bloom incidents within the reservoir, and the need to perform a multi-seasonal baseline inventory of aquatic plant species.

RECOMMENDED ACTION: The NRA is encouraged to work closely with the USGS Water Resources Division (Texas District), the USGS Biological Resources Division, TNRCC, IBWC, TPWD, the Bureau of Reclamation and appropriate universities in order to develop project proposals for synoptic studies or technical assistance requests to address the highest priority research issues identified as part of this scoping effort. A particularly viable source of funding for this type of research over the last several years has been the NPS/USGS Water Quality Partnership which has funded a number of intensive synoptic studies and technical assistance requests in a number of NPS units located in Texas. Information about this cooperative water quality partnership is available from Barry Long, NPS Water Resources Division (Fort Collins, CO) and Dr. Bruce Moring, USGS Water Resources Division (Austin, TX).

♦ **ASSESS THE POTENTIAL OF CURRENT AND POTENTIAL DEVELOPMENT / LAND USE CHANGE IN THE DEVILS RIVER WATERSHED ON SENSITIVE PARK RESOURCES** -- The Devils River watershed is the least impacted of all the major United States tributary streams flowing into the Lake Amistad Reservoir. It is also an area where increased pressures for growth and land use change are occurring.

RECOMMENDED ACTION: Because of its outstanding resource condition, and the increasing potential for land use change, it is recommended that Amistad NRA play an especially proactive role in influencing the management of this watershed. Recommended actions include: 1) undertake a comprehensive habitat evaluation and baseline inventory of aquatic species within the Devils River above the conservation pool level, 2) endorse increased water quality monitoring efforts within the Devils River watershed through both the Texas Clean Rivers Water Quality Monitoring Program and other efforts, 3) enhance involvement with regional planning activities with particular focus upon the Devils River watershed, and 4) explore opportunities for identifying and forwarding proposals for appropriate synoptic research studies to better define the water-related attributes of this important system.

♦ **ASSESS THE EFFECTS OF SEDIMENTATION ON VISITOR FACILITIES --** Sedimentation rates, particularly in the inflow areas of Amistad Reservoir, are thought to exceed expectations associated with the project design. Significant problems pertaining to shoaling, access to boat launch areas and access to the upper portions of the lake have resulted.

RECOMMENDED ACTION: Amistad NRA is encouraged to work with the International Boundary and Water Commission, the Bureau of Reclamation and the U.S. Geological Survey to design a study to both map and model sediment deposition on visitor access to important visitor facilities/use areas such as the Pecos River boat launch and Panther Cave. These studies should be used to begin to evaluate potential options for identifying and defining any appropriate mitigative options.

♦ **DEVELOP A PARKWIDE SPILL PREVENTION CONTROL AND COUNTER-MEASURE PLAN** -- Several significant transportation corridors (US 90, US 277/377, Union Pacific Railroad) occur in close proximity to the Amistad Reservoir. Additionally, three marinas provide fuelling services within the NRA. There is a potential for a petroleum or hazardous substances spill from these sources reaching the Amistad Reservoir.

RECOMMENDED ACTION: Based upon a moderate potential for a spill or other release of a potentially toxic or hazardous substance, it is recommended that Amistad NRA develop a Spill Prevention Control and Countermeasure Plan (SPCC). Such a plan should provide a description of contingency actions to be performed in the event of a spill or release including: 1) actions to secure the area to protect the public; 2) notification of appropriate agencies in the event of a spill or release; 3) spill containment actions including necessary equipment; and 4) cleanup/removal procedures and equipment.

♦ **SURVEY FOR AND INITIATE COOPERATIVE EFFORTS FOR THE CONTROL OF EXOTIC SPECIES** – Non-native species such as *hydrilla* are currently becoming established in Amistad and the Rio Grande. An exotic mammal, nutria has also become well established in the riparian area extending from Amistad Reservoir to Big Bend National Park and is thought to be damaging to riparian vegetation along the Rio Grande.

RECOMMENDED ACTION: The NRA should cooperate to the extent possible with the Bureau of Reclamation and/or Corps of Engineers in monitoring *hydrilla* within the NRA. The NRA should also work with Gerald McCrea of the NPS Santa Fe Intermountain Support Office and Pam Benjamin of the NPS Denver Intermountain Support Office in order to discuss options pertaining to the biological control of *hydrilla* and to develop appropriate funding proposals to assess the degree of impact of nutria upon native species and riparian vegetation within the NRA and to evaluate methods for the eradication or control of this species

♦ **SURVEY FOR KARST FEATURES FOUND ON PARK LANDS** - Thirty-two cave and sinkhole features have been documented at Amistad NRA. Many of these cave structures have been confirmed to be directly connected to the Amistad reservoir. Of the thirty-two known karst features, 18 have been surveyed. Most areas of the park need a baseline survey to confirm the presence of karst formations.

RECOMMENDED ACTION: All karst features around the reservoir should be mapped, with the information compiled in a database and associated GIS data layer. Information about each sinkhole should be gathered, including basic size and depth measurements, presence of water, sign of bat use or other animal use, presence of rare or unusual vegetation and signs of human use. Potential for pollution from trash, septic systems, road runoff, or other sources should be assessed. Maps of major sinkholes prior to reservoir construction created by BOR or IBWC should be investigated.

♦ **ACQUIRE COMPLETE KNOWLEDGE OF WATER QUANTITY ISSUES TO BE FACED IN NEXT 20 YEARS** - The Amistad Reservoir has been below conservation pool levels since 1993. Visitor access to many areas of the park are now inaccessible due to low lake levels. In the next 20 years, the human population in Texas is expected to reach 40 million. The water demands from domestic and industrial use along the Rio Grande are projected to increase significantly.

RECOMMENDED ACTION: Determine how international water treaties, previous 30 years of water management, future IBWC dam operation, and projected human populations will effect water levels at Amistad NRA. Produce recommendations for a low-water management plan that provides for alternatives in respect to cultural and natural resource protection and visitor use. Prepare new General Management Plan Statements that reflect the need to manage the NRA at low water levels.

♦ **ASSESS THE EFFECTS OF MOTORIZED VESSELS ON PARK RESOURCES** - Amistad NRA contains large numbers of motorized vessels on the reservoir. At Amistad NRA, the potential effects boat use on water resources are largely unknown. Excessive hydrocarbons produced by two-stroke engines, noise levels from boat engines, and boat congestion on the reservoir are all concerns.

RECOMMENDED ACTION: Determine the number of boats annually on Amistad Reservoir. Conduct water quality studies to document effects from two-stroke, 4-stroke, and jetfoot/PWC engines. Begin documenting visitor use levels at destination sites on the reservoir to determine visitor effects on resources.

REFERENCES

Anderson, B. 1974. An Archeological Assessment of Amistad Recreation Area Texas. Division of Archeology, Southwest Region, National Park Service. Sante Fe, New Mexico

Armstrong, A. W. 1995. The Use of Stable Isotope Ratios to Investigate the Relative Importance of Amistad Reservoir to Recharge of the McKnight and other associated Limestones, Southwestern Val Verde County, Texas, Master of Science, The University of Texas at San Antonio, Texas, 11/95 95pp.

Barker, R. A., P. W. Bush, and E. T. Baker, Jr.. 1994. Geologic History and Hydrogeologic Setting of the Edwards-Trinity Aquifer System, West Central Texas, U.S. Geological Survey, WRI Report 94-4039, Austin Texas, 51 pp.

R. E. Beck. 1991, ed., Waters and Water Rights 410, citing Tex. Water Code § 11.021.

Bestgen, K.R. and S.P. Platania. 1991. Status and Conservation of the Rio Grande Silvery Minnow, *Hybognathus amarus*. The Southwestern Naturalist. 36(2): 225-232.

Brune, Gunnar. 1975. Major and Historical Springs of Texas, Texas Water Development Board – Report 189, 94pp.

Brune, G. 1981. Springs of Texas. Volume 1. Branch-Smith, Inc. Fort Worth, Texas 76101.

Center, T.D. 1992. Biological Control of Weeds in Waterways and Public Lands in the Southeastern United States of America. In Proceedings, Vol. 1, First International Weed Control Congress, Melbourne Australia. Ed. J.H. Combellack, K.J. Levick, J. Parsons and R. G. Richardson.

ChemWaste. 1993. Draft Settlement Agreement and Scope of Work Between the National Park Service and Chemical Waste Management, Inc. dated November 29, 1993.

Clark, H.C. 1993. Technical Presentation on Geophysical Surveys Related to the Dryden Project in Santa Fe, NM on October 26, 1993.

Collins, M. B. and J. Labadie. 1999. The 1999 Texas Archeological Society Field School: Excavation, Rock Art Recordation, Surface Feature Documentation, and Survey at Amistad National Recreation Area. Texas Archeological Society Newsletter 43 (1):3-7. San Antonio, Texas.

Collins, M. B, J. Labadie, and E. R. Prewitt. 2000. A Brief Account of the 1999 TAS Field School, Amistad National Recreation Area. Texas Archeological Society Newsletter 44 (1): 9-17. San Antonio, Texas.

Christenson , P. K. 1981. Pecos River Well, Amistad National Recreation Area, NPS Water Resources Report 81-1, January 16, 1981.

Davis, W. B. and D. J. Schmidly. 1994. The Mammals of Texas. Texas Parks and Wildlife. Nongame and Urban Program. Austin, Texas.

Garrett, G.P., R.J. Edwards, and A.H. Price. 1992. Distribution and Status of the Devils River Minnow, *Dionda diaboli*. The Southwestern Naturalist 37(3): 259-267.

Garret, G. and J. Dean. 2001. Fish Species Checklist for Amistad NRA. Texas Parks and Wildlife Department. Inland Fisheries.

Golden, M. L., W. J. Gabriel, and J. W. Stevens, 1981. Soil Survey of Val Verde County, Texas, U.S. Department of Agriculture, Soil Conservation Service in cooperation with the Texas Agricultural Station and Val Verde County Commissioners Court, 64pp.

Gustavson, T. C. and M. B. Collins. 2000. An Assessment of Flood Damage to Archeological Sites in the San Pedro Drainage, Amistad National Recreation Area, August 1998. University of Texas at Austin, Texas Archeological Research Laboratory. Austin, Texas.

Haller, W.T., J.L. Miller and L.A. Garrard. 1976. Seasonal Production and germination of Hydrilla vegetative Propagules. J. Aquatic Plant Management. 14:26-29.

Harrell, H.L. 1978. Response of the Devils River (Texas) Fish Community to Flooding. Copeia 1978:60-68.

Howells, R.G. 1998. Freshwater Mussels of the Rio Grande with Special Emphasis on the Big Bend Region (Training Manual prepared for Big Bend national Park) . Texas Parks and Wildlife Department, Heart of the Hills Research Station, Ingram, TX, 19 pp.

International Boundary and Water Commission. 2001. Texas Clean Rivers Program Data. CD-ROM. Unpublished.

Intera. 1991. Chemical Waste Management, Inc.'s Permit Application for a Hazardous Waste Facility in Dryden, Texas. 12 volumes.

Intera. 1992. Revised Ground-Water Monitoring Report, Volume 10, Chapter V from Chemical Waste Management, Inc.'s Permit Application for a Hazardous Waste Management Facility in Dryden, Texas. 23 pp.

Jennings, S. 1998. Needs in the Management of Native Freshwater Mussels in the National Park System. Technical Report 97/147. Water Resources Division, National Park Service, Fort Collins, CO. 35 pp.

Jensen, R. 1987. Pecos River Fish Kills. Texas Water Resources Volume 13 Number 1: Spring 1987.

Jones and Neuse, Inc. 1991. Reasonable Worst-Case Emergency Analysis for Waste Management Facility, Dryden, Texas. 49 pp.

Kelly, M. E. 2001. The Rio Conchos, A Preliminary Overview. Texas Center for Policy Studies, Austin, TX. 27pp.

Labadie, J. H. 1994. Amistad National Recreation Area: A Cultural Resources Study. National Park Service, Southwest Cultural Resources Center. Santa Fe, New Mexico.

Labadie, J. H. 1999. Cultural Resources Management at the Amistad National Recreation Area, Del Rio, Texas. La Tierra, Journal of the South Texas Archeological Association, Vol. 26 (1): 18-23. San Antonio, Texas.

Langeland, K.A. 1996. *Hydrilla verticillata* (L.F.) Royle (Hydrocharitaceae), The Perfect Aquatic Weed. Castanea 61:293-304.

Larson, D. 2000. Tern Survey Field Notes. Amistad NRA.

Lee, R.W. and J.T. Wilson. 1997. Trace Elements and Organic Compounds Associated with Riverbed Sediments in the Rio Grande/Rio Bravo Basin, Mexico and Texas. U.S. Geological Survey Fact Sheet FS-098-97, 6 pp.

Lurry, D. 2000. Work Plan for the Rio Grande NASQAN Program, 2001-2005. USGS, Austin, TX. 11 pp.

Memorandum of Agreement between the United States Section, International Boundary and Water Commission and the National Park Service Relating to the Development and Administration of Recreation on the United States Side of Amistad International Dam and Reservoir. November 11, 1965.

Miyamoto, S, L.B., Fenn, D. Swietlik. 1995. Flow, Salts, and Trace Elements in the Rio Grande: A Review, Texas A&M University, Texas Water Resources Institute, TR-169, 30 pp.

Miyamota, S, M. Borah, A. Chacon, and R. Muttiah. 1999. Streamflow and Salinity Relationships in a Semi-Arid Watershed: A Case Study of the Rio Grande above Amistad. In Publication. Texas A&M University. 24 pp.

Moring, J.B.. 1999, Use of semipermeable membrane devices (SPMD) To Assess The Occurrence and Estimate Water Concentrations of Selected Organic Compounds in the Rio Grande from Presidio to Brownsville, Texas, U.S. Geological Survey Fact Sheet FS-100-99, 6 pp.

Mungall E. C. and W. J. Sheffield. 1994. Exotics on the Range, The Texas Example. Texas A&M University Press: College Station.

National Climate Data Center. 2000. World Climate 2000. TD 9641 Clim 81 1961-1996.

National Park Service. 1987. General Management Plan and Development Concept Plan. Amistad NRA. National Park Service, 104 pp .

National Park Service. 1993. Letter to the Texas Natural Resource Conservation Commission from the Regional Director of the Southwest Region dated November 8, 1993. 2 pp.

National Park Service. 1999a. Amistad National Recreation Area Park Map and Visitor Information Brochure. 2 pp.

National Park Service. 1999b. Reference Manual to Director's Order 83 - Public Health. National Park Service, Washington, DC. Appendix D (Bathing Beaches).

National Park Service. 1999c. March 3, 1999 Memo from Chief of Water Rights Branch to Field Solicitor, Sante Fe, NM. 2pp + attachments.

National Science and Technology Council). 2000. National Assessment of Harmful Algal Blooms in US Waters, 10 pp.

Nelson, S.M., G. Mueller, and D.C. Hemphill. 1994. Identification of Tire Leachate Toxicants and a Risk Assessment of Water Quality Effects using Tire Reefs in Canals. Bulletin of Environmental Contamination and Toxicology (1994) 52:57 pp574-581.

Niemi, E. and T. McGuckin. 1997. 1997 Water Management Study: Upper Rio Grande Basin Final Report to the Western Water Policy Review Advisory Commission.

Powell, A.M. 1994. Grasses of the Trans-Pecos and Adjacent Areas. University of Texas Press, Austin.

Powell, A.M. 1998. Trees and Shrubs of the Trans-Pecos and Adjacent Areas. University of Texas Press, Austin.

Public Law 101-682. 1990. Establishment of Amistad National Recreation Area. November 28, 1990.

Rees, R. and A.W. Buckner. 1980. Occurrence and Quality of Ground Water in the Edwards-Trinty (Plateau) Aquifer in the Trans-Pecos Region of Texas. 25 pp.

Reeves, R.D. and T.A. Small. 1973. Groundwater Resources of Val Verde County, Texas, Texas Water Development Board, Report 172.

Schmidt, James C. 1983. How to Identify and Control Water Weeds and Algae, 4th Edition, Applied Biochemists, Inc., 108 pp.

Schmidt, J.C., and B.L. Everitt. 2000. Hydrologic and geomorphic history of the Rio Grande/Rio Bravo between Fort Quitman and Amistad Reservoir and implications for river restoration, In Proceedings of the Rio Grande/Rio Bravo Symposium, 14 pp.

Shaffer, B. S, J. P. Dering, J. Labadie, and F. B. Pearl. 1997. Bioturbation at Submerged Cultural Sites by the Asiatic Clam: A Case Study from Amistad Reservoir, SW Texas. Journal of Field Archeology 24 (1): 135-138. Boston, MA.

Shaffer, B.S. and J.P Dering, J. Labadie, F.B. Pearl, A.M. Huebner. 1997. Bioturbation of Submerged Sites by the Asiatic Clam: A Case Study from Amistad Reservoir, SW Texas. Texas A&M University. College Station, Texas.

Shertz, T.L. 1990. Trends in Water-Quality Data in Texas, U.S. Geological Survey Water-Resources Investigations Report 89-4178, 177 pp.

Shertz, T.L., F.C . Wells, and D.J. Ohe,. 1994. Sources of Trends in Water-Quality Data for Selected Streams in Texas, U.S. Geological Survey Water-Resources Investigations Report 94-4213, 49 pp.

Sidle, J. G. and W.F. Harrison. 1990. Recovery Plan for the Interior Population of the Least Tern. Department of the Interior. U.S. Fish and Wildlife Service.

Smith, C.I., G. P. Bolden, R. E. Webster, and J. B. Brown. 1983. Structure and Stratigraphy of the ValVerde Basin- Devils River Uplift, Texas, West Texas Geological Society Publication #83-77, 26pp.

Sorola, S. 1988. Interior Least Tern survey of Amistad Reservoir. TX Parks and Wildlife. Del Rio, TX.

Spearing, Darwin. 1991. Roadside Geology of Texas, Mountain Press Publishing Company, Missoula, Montana, pp. 137-144.

Texas Natural Heritage Program. 1993. Plant Communities of Texas (Series Level). Wildlife Diversity Program. Texas Parks and Wildlife. Austin, TX

Texas Natural Heritage Program. 1995. Biological Survey of Amistad Reservoir Recreation Site. Final Report. Texas Parks and Wildlife Department. 3000 South Interstate 35, Suite 100. Austin, TX 78704.

Texas Natural Resource Conservation Commission. 1994a. Regional Assessment of Water Quality in the Rio Grande Basin: Texas Natural Resource Conservation Commission, 377 pp.

Texas Natural Resource Conservation Commission. 1994b. Binational Study Regarding the Presence of Toxic Substances in The Rio Grande/Rio Bravo and Its Tributaries Along its Boundary Portions Between the United States and Mexico: Texas Natural Resource Conservation Commission, 246 pp.

Texas Natural Resource Conservation Commission. 2000. Texas Surface Water Quality Standards: Texas Administrative Code, Title 30, Chapter 307.2-307.10, August 2000, 157 pp.

Texas Natural Resource Conservation Commission. 1996a. 1996 Regional Assessment of Water Quality in the Rio Grande Basin. TNRCC. 74pp.

Texas Natural Resource Conservation Commission. 1996b. The State of Texas Water Quality Inventory. Volume 4, 13th edition. Report No. SFR-50, Austin, TX.

Texas Natural Resource Conservation Commission. 1997. Second Phase of the Binational Study Regarding The Presence of Toxic Substances in the Rio Grande/Rio Bravo and its Tributaries Along its Boundary Portions Between the United States and Mexico: Texas Natural Resource Conservation Commission, 246 pp.

Texas Natural Resource Conservation Commission. 1999. 1999 Clean Water Act Section 303(d) List and Schedule for Development of Total Maximum Daily Loads (TMDLs) SFR-58/99, http://www.tnrcc.state.tx.us/admin/topdoc/sfr/058-99/index.html.

Texas Natural Resource Conservation Commission. 2000. 2000 Clean Water Act Section 303(d) List (Final Draft). Web Site www.tnrcc.state.tx.us/water/quality/00_303d.html

Texas Water Commission. 1992. Regional Assessment Of Water Quality In The Rio Grande Basin: Texas Water Commission, 207 pp.

Van Metre, P.C., B.J. Mahler, and E. Calendar. 1997. Water-quality trends in the Rio Grande/Rio Bravo Basin using Sediment Cores from Reservoirs: U.S. Geological Survey Fact Sheet FS-221-96, 8 pp.

U.S. Census Bureau, Internet Release April 2, 2001. http://www.census.gov/population/cen2000/phc-t4/tab04.pdf

U.S. Department of the Interior. 2000. Development of an International Cooperative Fisheries Management Plan for Amistad Reservoir. Project Proposal prepared by the National Park Service, Amistad NRA, Del Rio, TX and U.S. Fish and Wildlife Service, Austin, TX. 5 pp. + attachments.

U.S. Fish and Wildlife Service. 1995. Threatened and Endangered Species of Texas. Department of the Interior. U.S. Fish and Wildlife Service. Ecological Services Field Office. Austin, TX.

U.S. Fish and Wildlife Service. 1999. Federally listed as Threatened and Endangered Species of Texas. Val Verde County, Texas. December 2, 1999

U.S. Geological Survey. 1999a. NASQAN Data - Rio Grande Basin 1996-1998. Pecos River near Langtry, Texas (08447410). June, 1999 http://water.usgs.gov/nasqan/data/finaldata/pecos.html

U.S. Geological Survey. 1999B. NASQAN Data - Rio Grande Basin 1996-1998. Foster Ranch near Langtry, Texas (08377200). June, 1999. http://water.usgs.gov/nasqan/data/finaldata/foster.html

U.S. Geological Survey. 2000. Summary Statistics for NASQAN Data--Rio Grande Basin 1996-1999. http://water.usgs.gov/nasqan/data/statsum.html

U.S. Geological Survey. 2001. Water Resources Data, Texas Water Year 2000. Volume 5. Guadalupe River Basin, Nueces River Basin, Rio Grande Basin, and Intervening Coastal Basins. Water Data Report TX-00-5, U.S. Geological Survey, Austin, TX. 385 pp.

Zerr, R. W. 2000. 1999 Survey Report for Amistad Reservoir. Statewide Freshwater Fisheries Monitoring and Management Program, Texas Parks and Wildlife Department, Inland Fisheries Division, District I-D, San Antonio, TX. 22 pp.

Appendix 1: List of Abbreviations Used in this Report

ac-ft	acre-feet
BOR	Bureau of Reclamation
IBWC	International Boundary and Water Commission
cfs	cubic feet per second
cms	cubic meters per second
CNA	Comision Nacional del Aqua
CRP	Clean Rivers Program
km	kilometers
gpm	gallons per minute
m	meters
mg/l	milligrams per liter
MTBE	Methyl Tertiary Butyl Ether
NASQAN	National Stream Quality Accounting Program
NEPA	National Environmental Policy Act
NPS	National Park Service
NRA	National Recreation Area
PCB	Polychlorinated Biphenyls
PWC	Personal Water Craft
SEGARPA	Secretariat of Agriculture, Livestock, Rural Development, Fisheries, and Nutrition
SEMARNAP	Secretariat of Environment, Natural Resources and Fisheries (now know as SEMARNAT)
SEMARNAT	Secretariat of Environment, Natural Resources (SEMARNAT).
SOF	Statement of Findings
SPCC	Spill Prevention Control and Countermeasure Plan
SQWM	Surface Water Quality Monitoring Program
TNHP	Texas Natural Heritage Program
TNRCC	Texas Natural Resource Conservation Commission
TPWD	Texas Parks and Wildlife Department
USGS	United States Geological Survey
USEPA	United States Environmetal Protection Agency
USFWS	United States Fish and Wildlife Service

Appendix 2: Amistad NRA Checklist Of Fish Species:

Scientific name	Common name	Occurrence
Lepisosteus oculatus	spotted gar	present
Lepisosteus osseus	longnose gar	present
Lepisosteus spatula	alligator gar	present
Dorosoma cepedianum	gizzard shad	abundant
Dorosoma petenense	threadfin shad	abundant
Carassius auratus	goldfish	rare
Cyprinella lutrensis	red shiner	abundant
Cyprinella proserpina	proserpine shiner	present
Cyprinella venusta	blacktail shiner	abundant
Cyprinus carpio	common carp	abundant
Dionda argentosa	manantial roundnose minnow	abundant
Dionda diaboli	Devils River minnow	rare
Dionda episcopa	roundnose minnow	present
Macrhybopsis aestivalis	speckled chub	rare
Notemigonus crysoleucas	golden shiner	present
Notropis amabilis	Texas shiner	abundant
Notropis braytoni	Tamaulipas shiner	abundant
Notropis chihuahua	Chihuahua shiner	rare
Notropis jemezanus	Rio Grande shiner	rare
Notropis stramineus	sand shiner	abundant
Pimephales vigilax	bullhead minnow	abundant
Rhinichthys cataractae	longnose dace	rare
Carpiodes carpio	river carpsucker	abundant
Cycleptus elongatus	blue sucker	rare
Ictiobus bubalus	smallmouth buffalo	abundant
Moxostoma austrinum	west Mexican redhorse	rare
Moxostoma congestum	gray redhorse	abundant
Astyanax mexicanus	Mexican tetra	abundant
Ameiurus natalis	yellow bullhead	present
Ictalurus furcatus	blue catfish	present
Ictalurus lupus	headwater catfish	rare
Ictalurus punctatus	channel catfish	abundant
Noturus gyrinus	tadpole madtom	rare
Pylodictis olivaris	flathead catfish	abundant
Cyprinodon eximius	Conchos pupfish	rare
Cyprinodon hybrids	sheepshead minnow x Pecos pupfish	rare
Fundulus grandis	Gulf killifish	present
Gambusia affinis	western mosquitofish	present
Gambusia geiseri	largespring gambusia	present
Gambusia senilis	blotched gambusia	extirpated
Gambusia speciosa	Mexican mosquitofish	abundant

Scientific name	Common name	Occurrence
Poecilia latipinna	sailfin molly	present
Menidia beryllina	inland silverside	abundant
Morone chrysops	white bass	abundant
Morone saxatilis	striped bass	abundant
Lepomis auritus	redbreast sunfish	abundant
Lepomis cyanellus	green sunfish	abundant
Lepomis gulosus	warmouth	abundant
Lepomis macrochirus	bluegill	abundant
Lepomis megalotis	longear sunfish	present
Lepomis microlophus	redear sunfish	present
Micropterus dolomieu	smallmouth bass	present
Micropterus salmoides	largemouth bass	abundant
Pomoxis annularis	white crappie	present
Etheostoma grahami	Rio Grande darter	present
Percina caprodes	logperch	abundant
Stizostedion vitreum	walleye	rare
Aplodinotus grunniens	freshwater drum	present
Cichlasoma cyanoguttatum	Rio Grande cichlid	present
Oreochromis aureus	blue tilapia	present

From Garret and Dean, 2001.

As the nation's principal conservation agency, the Department of the Interior has responsibility for most of our nationally owned public lands and natural resources. This includes fostering sound use of our land and water resources; protecting our fish, wildlife, and biological diversity; preserving the environmental and cultural values of our national parks and historical places; and providing for the enjoyment of life through outdoor recreation. The department assesses our energy and mineral resources and works to ensure that their development is in the best interests of all our people by encouraging stewardship and citizen participation in their care. The department also has a major responsibility for American Indian reservation communities and for people who live in island territories under U.S. administration.

NPS D-53, September 2001